Adult education in changing times

Adult education in changing times

Policies, philosophies and professionalism

Marion Bowl

promoting adult learning

Published by

© 2014 National Institute of Adult Continuing Education (England and Wales)
21 De Montfort Street, Leicester, LE1 7GE

Company registration no. 2603322
Charity registration no. 1002775

The National Institute of Adult Continuing Education (NIACE) is an
independent charity which promotes adult learning across England and Wales.
Through its research, development, publications, events, outreach and advocacy
activity, NIACE works to improve the quality and breadth of opportunities
available for all adults so they can benefit from learning throughout their lives.

www.niace.org.uk

For details of all our publications, visit http://shop.niace.org.uk

Cataloguing in Publications Data

A CIP record for this title is available from the British Library

978-1-86201-650-7 (print)
978-1-86201-651-4 (PDF)
978-1-86201-652-1 (ePub)
978-1-86201-653-8 (Kindle)

All websites referenced in this book were correct and accessible at the time of
going to press.

Printed in the UK by Marston Book Services, Abingdon.
Cover design by Book Production Services, London.
Typeset by Avon DataSet Ltd, Bidford on Avon, Warwickshire, UK.

The views expressed in this publication are not necessarily endorsed by the
publisher.

Contents

Acknowledgements

Central to this book are the perspectives of adult educators in England and New Zealand who were willing to give up their time to be interviewed about their careers and their perspectives on adult education. Their names have been altered to protect their identities but I am extremely grateful for their assistance.

In New Zealand, Robert Tobias and Jennifer Leahy have been inspirational adult educators and academics whose wisdom and encouragement have been invaluable throughout the process of writing this book. In England, Tim Davies has been a constant source of support and feedback, a very patient advisor, editor and friend. In addition, I am grateful to Jane Martin for her thoughtful and constructive feedback on the first draft of this book.

My thanks go to The Universities and Colleges Union (UCU) and the ESOL research network (in England) and to ACE Aotearoa (in New Zealand) for help with contacting adult educators. Finally, Joel Lazarus, Bernard Godding and Margaret Humphries provided me with insights about historical and recent developments in the field. Thanks to them for their hospitality and willingness to share their knowledge.

Notwithstanding all the support and assistance I have been grateful to receive, any errors or omissions are my own.

Introduction

Adult learning is relevant to personal empowerment, economic well-being, community cohesion and societal development. As a sector adult education contributes to alleviating poverty and unemployment, skilling the workforce, stemming the spread of HIV and AIDS, preserving and sustaining the environment, raising awareness of human rights, combating racism and xenophobia, supporting democratic values and active citizenship and strengthening gender equity and equality. (UNESCO, 2009: 43)

Adult educators too often suffer from low status and remuneration, affecting the quality and sustainability of programmes. Sufficient, predictable and well-targeted funding is more the exception than the rule. (UNESCO, 2009: 9)

Two questions frustrate many longstanding adult educators in Europe, North America, Australia, New Zealand and elsewhere. Why, when lifelong learning has been a policy priority for the past 40 years, does publicly funded adult education appear to be fighting for its life? And why do so many qualified, skilled and experienced adult educators find themselves in an educational landscape that does not recognise or value their contribution? Much has been written about lifelong learning since the term became global shorthand for a range of educational purposes, policies and projects. Much, too, has been written about the ways in which neoliberalism has reshaped lifelong learning for its own

1

economistic ends. However, less attention has been paid to the impact of these developments on adult educators themselves and on the ways in which they interpret their purpose, carry out their work and seek to resist or accommodate the dominant global policy orthodoxy. Through this book I explore the realities of adult educators' practice against the background of the current political and economic climate, discuss the challenges that adult educators face, and suggest some of the theories and strategies that might help to rescue adult education and direct it towards social justice and equality as well as the development of political awareness.

Neoliberalism and its impact on adult education

Since the mid-1970s neoliberalising discourses and policies have been radically re-shaping the field of education (Gordon and Whitty, 1997; Bourdieu, 1998; Apple, 2000, 2001; Harvey, 2005) and adult education has become enmeshed in these policies (Foley, 1999; Martin, 2006: Zepke, 2009; Bowl, 2010). The logic of neoliberalism is underpinned by a conviction that economic relations and the 'discipline of the market' are paramount and that the state should take a minimal role in the social realm. This, it is argued, will produce benefits for the national economy and develop human capital (Becker, 1975) which, in turn, will fuel economic competitiveness.

Influenced by this general shift to consumerism and instrumentalism in education, a number of assumptions have become commonplace in adult education policy and practice. The first is that, as far as possible, individuals should pay for their own education. A policy of 'user pays' has been applied in much of the post-compulsory education sector, leading to raised fee levels and reduced subsidies. As government subsidies for non-vocational adult education have been cut, many community-based adult education classes have closed, unable to support their continuation through learner-funded courses.

The second assumption is that government support for educating adults should serve primarily economic ends; hence the emphasis on training for work, vocational skills and employability, rather than a broader view of adult education for social as well as individual development (Coffield, 1999, 2000). The third assumption is that adults deemed to be lacking 'functional' or 'employability' skills should be the prime targets of education and training interventions. The very notion of 'post-

2

compulsory' education has been undermined by the trend for adult education and training to be seen as a condition for employability and, thus, social inclusion (Crowther, 2004; M. Ball, 2009).

Hand in hand, though in apparent contradiction with the free-market rhetoric of neoliberalism, new managerialism and the culture of performativity have also been brought to bear on educators' work (S. Ball, 2000; Apple, 2000, 2001; Gewirtz and Ball, 2000; Thrupp and Willmott, 2003; Wilkins *et al.*, 2012). Justified as a means of driving up quality, performative systems are characterised by an audit-driven culture in which data collection and outcomes measurement are foregrounded as ways of judging the performance of both learners and teachers and the notion of professional judgement, arrived at in the process of dialogue with colleagues and learners, is abandoned in favour of externally-imposed measurements of performance, enforced by management threats and sanctions (Seddon, 1997; S. Ball, 2003, 2012). Performative regimes, as described by Stephen Ball, will be familiar to those adult educators who battle to balance their professional judgements about teaching and the climate of the classroom with the demands of audit and the increasing bureaucratisation of their work:

> ... *a powerful and insidious policy technology that is now at work at all levels and in all kinds of education and public service, a technology that links effort, values, purposes and self-understanding to measures and comparisons of output. Within the rigours and disciplines of performativity we are required to spend increasing amounts of our time in making ourselves accountable, reporting on what we do rather than doing it.* (S. Ball, 2012: 19)

The result of this trend has been the imposition of qualification frameworks, outcomes-based assessments, audits and inspections – which have long been commonplace in the field of schooling – in many areas of adult education (Lawy and Tedder, 2009; Fenwick, 2010; Govers, 2010). In some contexts (for example in community-based adult education in New Zealand) these developments arrived quite recently and suddenly; in others (for example in English further education colleges) they have been part of the territory of educational work with adults for 20 years.

The recognition of adult education as an organised – and paid – field of practice came relatively late compared with school education. Until education and training for skills and employability became a policy priority from the late 1970s onward, the contribution of adult education to the development of society, communities and individuals was not widely marked by policy makers. This has had both positive and negative implications. On the positive side, adult educators have enjoyed some freedom to work outside the more rigid structures of formal educational institutions: there has been room for creative practice, flexibility to innovate and potential to engage with individuals and communities for the purposes of social action as well as individual accreditation and employability. Work in adult education has offered space for those committed to more radical political and social goals to work together with individuals and communities in settings where, although learning certainly takes place, it may not be foregrounded as such. However, this marginality has its negative side. Few of those who work in the field of adult education can regard it as a 'career'; it has a long tradition of voluntary, casualised, temporary and hourly paid employment. Routes into adult education work tend to be haphazard and ill-defined and prospects for a permanent living wage are not good for newcomers.

Government investment in adult education has tended to be low compared with that for school-based education and is particularly prone to buffeting by political and economic winds. Not surprisingly, the financial crises since 2008 in Europe, North America, Australia and New Zealand have precipitated policies of fiscal restraint which have had a negative impact on adult education, further diminishing it as field of practice, except where it is clearly tied into instrumental policy aims, and worsening adult educators' conditions of employment and job prospects. The first purpose of this book is to examine the impact of changes in global policy on adult education as a field of practice.

While global shifts in the way education is viewed are undeniably affecting adult education, history and culture as well as socioeconomic circumstances are likely to influence the extent to which adult education is prioritised and resourced at a national level and the type of work in which adult educators are engaged (Rust, 2000). A second aim of this book is therefore to compare developments in adult education in two countries – England and New Zealand – which share aspects of a common history, based in colonialism and Eurocentric domination, but also demographic and cultural differences resulting from historical forces and struggles (Walker, 1990; Tobias, 1994; Thrupp, 2001).

Adult educators' practice is not only influenced by international

4

and national discourses and policies, however. Adult educators' ideas about the aims of education are also likely to have been shaped by their biographies, their educational backgrounds and their personal and professional experiences, as well as those of their peers. This book explores how adult educators – their values, their work, their expectations and the expectations laid upon them – are being affected by the changing political and economic environment. A particular concern is to assess the extent to which adult educators can continue to exercise professional agency and judgement in the current context, to work against the grain of policies and practices which conflict with their values or which they feel are not in the interests of adult learners and communities. Finally, the book draws lessons from the efforts of adult education practitioners and organisations to rescue and keep alive a broader vision of adult and community education as a vehicle for social development and political change in the face of increasingly instrumental and marketised policy hegemony.

Mapping the field of adult education

Merriam and Brockett describe adult education as involving:

> ... *activities intentionally designed for the purpose of bringing about learning among those whose age, social roles or self-perception define them as adults.* (1997: 8)

This definition suggests that adult education, like school education, is planned and purposeful. In addition, it implies a role for the educator: to facilitate and encourage the process of learning. The inference is, too, that there is something about adult learners – the fact that they have undergone a maturation process and/or that they have accrued experience through life and work – which differentiates their learning from that of school-age students.

However, in practice the field of adult and community education is not easily delineated (Tobias, 1996a; Merriam and Brockett, 1997; Osborne and Sankey, 2009; Rubenson, 2010). Adult education activities may take place in a diverse range of contexts, from formally organised and accredited programmes within large and generalist educational institutions (such as in tertiary education colleges and universities) to loosely organised and non-accredited activity within informal groupings, such as community or work-based organisations and group learning for leisure, personal interest or political and social education.

The idea that adults, because of their maturity and their experience of life and work, can be considered as a different 'species' of learner requiring a specifically adult teaching approach (Knowles, 1973) has been widely contested. Knowles premised the concept of 'andragogy' on certain assumptions:

- that adults, as they mature, become increasingly capable of self-direction and therefore more able (with guidance from the adult educator) to assess their own learning needs;
- that adults have quantitatively and qualitatively more experience than younger people. On the one hand, this may mean they have a richer foundation on which to build knowledge and share with others; on the other it may mean that they are more firmly attached to fixed beliefs and habits of learning which the adult educator may need to challenge;
- that adults' 'readiness to learn' is oriented to the fulfillment of social roles – particularly those related to work;
- that adults are drawn to problem-centred learning, which links to their immediate context, rather than subject-based knowledge oriented to the future.

These assumptions have been criticised on a number of grounds (Brookfield, 1986; Hanson, 1996). The first of these is the difficulty of determining at what point an individual changes from being other-directed to being self-directed or, indeed, whether it is true to say that younger people are not able to be self-directed learners. Second, it does not seem to be the case that experiential learning is the *sine qua non* for adults. There are clearly circumstances in which experiential learning is neither preferred nor appropriate for adults. Third, Knowles's tendency towards instrumentalism – the view that adult education should be organised around immediate and practical learning needs – flies in the face of a liberal adult education philosophy that promotes the benefits of learning for personal fulfilment, and radical perspectives which see the potential of learning as a means to bring about social change. Knowles's notion of learner-readiness is also undermined by the tendency in recent years in many industrialised countries for some forms of adult education and training to be overtly or tacitly obligatory. For example, in some

6

instances, training for work and the development of 'employability skills' have become a condition of receiving state benefits (Preston, 1999), parenting education has been proposed as way of preventing child abuse and neglect and the 'empowering' effects of adult education have been advocated in criminal justice and substance abuse contexts (Hannah-Moffatt, 2000).

Given these definitional difficulties, it is tempting to wonder whether adult education can really be seen as a field of practice in its own right. Why cannot adult education be simply subsumed within the general field of lifelong learning? Alternatively, why should training for work, adult literacy and language, community-based classes and continuing professional development not be regarded as separate and unrelated fields? I offer three reasons. First, whatever the differences in settings and roles, there do appear to be certain principles and values underlying adult educators' work that relate to their perception of the particular needs of adults. Second, adults (however loosely defined) experience economic, political, social and personal circumstances which they can be facilitated to address and challenge through adult education and the efforts of adult educators. Third, some of the approaches that have been advocated by adult education practitioners and theorists continue to offer lessons for formal schooling and challenge some of the taken-for-granted assumptions of formal education (Harber, 2009). Adult education as discussed in this book therefore refers to education which focuses on:

- second chance education for those who, for whatever reason, did not progress educationally beyond compulsory schooling and who wish to do so;
- alternative educational provision which validates those experiences not privileged in school education;
- education for specific groups of adults (for example, new migrants) whose personal and social situations would be enhanced thereby;
- community-based and informal education for personal, social or community development and change; and
- education for non-vocational aims.

However, reflecting perhaps the shifting policy focus of educational activity with adults, it is recognised that the line between adult education and training for and in work has become increasingly blurred.

The scope and nature of adult educators' work

As the foregoing discussion suggests, adult education is a fragmented field of practice (Field, 2000; Boud and Rooney, 2010), spanning activity from basic literacy and numeracy to university continuing education. UNESCO's (2009) *Global Report on Adult Learning and Education* has painted a picture of the types of work in which adult educators across the world may be engaged. Basic education (mainly literacy) remains the most common form of adult education (82 per cent of 127 countries declaring that as an area in which they are engaged). This is closely followed by vocational and work-related education (76 per cent of countries stating this as an area in which they are active). In addition, adult education may be offered in settings as diverse as community meeting places, schools, colleges and universities, health centres and prisons. Because of this diversity of purpose and context, those organising and teaching in adult education may be more likely to identify with the particular context in which they work – for example in a community setting, in the health sector or in a polytechnic or college of further education – rather than identifying themselves as operating in a field of adult education practice (Tobias, 1996a; Merriam and Brockett, 1997). Thus adult educators may refer to themselves or be referred to as: lecturer, teacher, trainer, tutor, instructor, mentor or facilitator. There is a tendency for descriptions of adult educators to be context specific; for example, in an informal setting the adult educator may call herself a 'facilitator'; in some community development settings the term 'animateur' has been utilised to emphasise the facilitative, catalytic nature of the adult educator's work, contrasting it with the more didactic connotations of 'teacher' or 'lecturer'. Increasingly, 'tutor' is used in formal adult education settings as a blanket term which covers both formal teaching and less formal one-to-one or group guidance and support for learning. Each designation reflects a slightly different perspective on the nature and purpose of the adult educator's work.

At the same time, those who work as adult educators may not regard it as their primary professional identity. They may, for example, be working in another full-time professional role, fitting in teaching adult education evening classes, weekend and summer schools with other careers in or outside teaching, supporting or supplementing their income from their main area of expertise. For example, it is not uncommon for those in the creative professions to be teaching art, music or creative writing as a means of making ends meet in a precarious occupation.

> *...many of those working in adult education are 'moonlighting'*
> *– that is, gainfully employed in second jobs, with their main*
> *employment as teachers in the formal school system. Consequently*
> *many working in the sector have difficulties developing a professional*
> *identity and primary commitment as adult educator; many others*
> *do not recognise themselves as genuinely belonging to the sector.*
> (UNESCO, 2009: 93)

Finally, the developing tendency to talk about adult learning rather than adult education reflects a discourse of lifelong learning which separates the educator from the cognitive process (Field, 2000), with the implication that the learner is viewed as autonomous and capable of self-direction in all learning. Knowles's (1973) notion of the 'self-directed' learner has thus been put to the service of policies which have tended to write the educator out of the equation. However, as this book will demonstrate, there is still a sizable cohort of people who regard themselves as educators of adults in a range of settings and for a range of individual and social purposes – and they regard their contribution to adults' individual, community and social development as important.

Situating adult educators' beliefs and values

In the field of adult education, perhaps more than in schooling, discussion of the beliefs and values that inform educational practice has featured strongly. Such discussion typically concerns the ideas that underlie adult education's purposes, curricula, teacher–learner relationships and methods of teaching and assessment. As will be seen later in this book, although adult educators may be reluctant to explicitly articulate their philosophies of education, their motivations and priorities are likely to be underpinned by values and beliefs about the purposes and aims of education. There is a wealth of literature (discussed in Merriam and Brockett, 1997) which suggests that adult educators align to discrete philosophical positions, each with its own theoretical stance towards and view of the learner, learning and the educator. These positions have arisen from particular historical, political and social circumstances. Apps (1973), Heimstra (1988), Zinn (1990) and Elias and Merriam (1994) identify five main philosophical traditions: liberal, behaviourist, progressive, humanist and radical, whose positions may be summarised thus:

- *Liberal*: concerned with the development of an informed, cultured and moral citizenry and with the value of knowledge acquisition 'for its own sake'. The adult educator is characterised as the conveyor of an established body of knowledge.
- *Behaviourist*: concerned with behaviour change and the acquisition of competence in prescribed areas, for the better functioning of the individual, the economy or society. The adult educator is characterised as managing the 'delivery' of prescribed educational or behavioural outcomes.
- *Progressive:* concerned with the development of practical problem-solving skills which enable the learner to act upon and change society. The adult educators' role is seen as that of organiser, guide and evaluator of the learning process.
- *Humanistic:* concerned with personal growth and development and self-actualisation. The adult educator acts as facilitator and resource for learning.
- *Radical*: concerned with education's role in bringing about funda-mental social, economic and political change. The adult educator is characterised as catalyst for and facilitator of collective thought and action.

These positions are rooted in particular moments in the history of struggles for knowledge and power and thus linked to specific strands of the adult education movement. While it might be hypothesised that individual adult educators working on a day-to-day basis will take a more pragmatic approach than these categories suggest (Heimstra, 1988), that they may not be comfortable with articulating a philosophical position (Cranton, 1994) and that such categorisations are in any case over-simplified, it does raise the question – discussed in this book – of how adult educators act in situations where the dominant policy thrust is at odds with their own values and beliefs. What happens, as is currently the case, when policy shifts marginalise a radical, liberal or humanist perspective and promote more instrumentalist ends? For example, how are adult educators reconciling a concern for equal access to education with the development of an educational market? How do they promote an open-ended, dialogical approach to learning when faced with prescribed learning outcomes and accreditation regimes? To what extent are adult educators able to draw on adult education philosophies and theories to articulate alternatives and mobilise to resist dominant discourses and policies? Or are the conditions in which they work so constrained that their only option is to capitulate to or assimilate the dominant ideologies underpinning current policies?

Professionalism and career identity in adult education

Another issue which has preoccupied writers and policy makers across a number of countries, including England and New Zealand, is the professional status of adult education (Merriam and Brockett, 1997; Tobias, 2003; Guimarães, 2009; Osborne and Sankey, 2009; Yee Fan Tang, 2011). Professional status, in the traditionally accepted use of the term (Flexner, 1915; Millerson, 1964; Eraut, 1994), is conferred on occupations which are viewed as performing a recognised social function requiring a high degree of specialised knowledge and skill and drawing on an ethical system which is autonomously regulated by the membership of that profession. The applicability of this elite conception of professionalism to education has been much debated (Etzioni, 1969; Gordon *et al.*, 1985; Tobias, 2003) and alternative conceptualisations have been proposed (Goodson and Hargreaves, 1996; Sachs, 2003) which imply a more reflective, democratic and less exclusive professional ethos. However, the issue of professionalism has also become bound up in government policies around education which have increasingly tended towards control and the surveillance of teacher performance (Beck, 2008, 2009; Fitzgerald, 2008).

For adult education is bound up in other issues too. First, while it may be argued that recognised professional status improves the standing of the individual worker and the field of adult education as a whole, the relatively low pay and job insecurity of adult educators make the issue of their professionalisation seem somewhat irrelevant. More pressing (as will be seen in Chapter Six) is the issue of what it means to try to sustain a career of any kind in adult education. Rather, it might be argued that adult educators, along with school teachers, are in the process of being de-professionalised through the implementation of regimes of managerial accountability. Second, while adult education can be said to meet the criterion of altruistic service, in all other respects its professional status is more questionable. Traditionally there has been no specific qualification requirement for adult educators. Some come from a school teaching background; others may possess particular skills and knowledge in their subject discipline. The range of routes to 'qualification' has been diverse and, while the desire for adult educators to be trained for their role may have become an increasing policy priority, this has not been reflected in an increase in opportunities or funding for practitioners to study adult education at higher levels. In New Zealand and England the policy debate around professionalism has tended to focus on standards and the requirement to undertake short-term and relatively low-level professional development and training. Finally, professional status is a thorny issue for adult educators whose aim is to break down the power differentials which typically separate professional elites from the mass of the population. It does not sit well with ideas of democracy and equality which so frequently infuse adult educators' narratives of empowerment. In this sense the policy preoccupation with professionalisation runs counter to the values of many adult educators. How these tensions between professional status and the ideals and realities of practice are manifested will be dealt with in more detail in later chapters.

Summary of the book

Section One charts the historical and political contexts for adult education, with particular reference to England and New Zealand, the two countries which are the focus of the research for this book. This introductory chapter has reviewed some of the current issues in adult education practice which will be reflected throughout the book: the nature and scope of adult educators' work; the values and philosophies which are said to underpin adult education practice; and the shape of adult education as a field of practice. Chapter One provides an overview of the changing policy discourse in adult education and lifelong learning at a global level, with particular reference to the role of UNESCO and other international organisations. Chapter Two draws on the historical and policy literature to offer an account of changing adult education policy and practice at national level in England and New Zealand. It illustrates the strength of the influence of global trends and ideologies in both countries, which has resulted in a degree of policy convergence. It suggests, however, that some aspects of policy continue to be influenced by the specificities of historical, national and cultural contexts and may therefore be amenable to change through local action. As Chapter Three explains, the debate around adult education and professionalism is a long-running one. However, it has taken on new intensity in the context of increasing managerialism in the post-compulsory education sector. The chapter focuses on attempts to prescribe training standards for adult educators in England and the policy push for professional development in New Zealand. It provides evidence of the contradictions of 'professionalisation' in the context of the continuing casualisation and increasing regulation of adult educators' work.

Section Two of the book draws on research conducted with 62 adult educators in England and New Zealand in 2011 and 2012. The research took a narrative, career biography approach to exploring these educators' careers and their views about practice in the current political and economic climate. Chapter Four provides a brief rationale for the research and a description of how it was conducted. Chapter Five presents adult educators' perspectives on the purposes of adult education. The interviews suggested a more fluid and complex picture of adult educators' philosophical alignments than is generally found in the literature. They also suggested a dominant orientation towards liberalism/ humanism and values of equality of opportunity and fairness, which does not sit well with current national policies in either England or New Zealand. The chapter highlights the reluctance of some adult educators explicitly to incorporate theory into their understanding of practice. I argue that one implication of this reluctance is that adult educators struggle to articulate a coherent sense of purpose, leaving them – and adult education as a field of practice – vulnerable to attack in hostile policy climates. Chapter Six explores the notion of a 'career' in adult education in the prevailing political and fiscal climate. It first examines how adult educators have typically entered and trained for the field of practice and the expectations placed upon them in their work. It goes on to discuss the impact of work intensification and contractual uncertainty on their working lives and contrasts this with the policy preoccupation of professionalisation and professional development discussed in Chapter Three. Chapter Seven describes how adult educators in England and New Zealand are managing the contradictions between their beliefs about adult education and the expectations placed upon them by policy. It discusses the tactics that adult educators adopt in practice in order to work in ways which are consistent with their values. It goes on to argue that tactics of 'micro resistance' may inadvertently perpetuate an illusion that working creatively in the 'spaces' between policy intentions and regimes of accountability will benefit adult education in the longer term. Chapter Eight takes the discussion beyond the dilemmas of the workplace and evaluates some of the strategic responses of practitioners and practitioner organisations to the policy climate. These responses range from fatalism to advocacy and campaigning and include the development of social entrepreneurial forms of adult education as a 'third way' for practice which attempts to reconcile social need and the market. The final chapter summarises the main themes of the book and the lessons they offer for practice, theory and action. Adult educators are still finding space to work against the grain of policy. However, their fate is inextricably linked with global political economy – a fact which needs to be explicitly acknowledged and critically explored. As such, their future lies in making common cause with others defending work in the public sphere within and outside their immediate context for work.

Section One

Historical and political contexts for adult education

CHAPTER ONE

From adult education to lifelong learning: A changing global landscape

Although historical research must necessarily devote considerable attention to the detailed study of the institutions, significant historical actors, and the development of public policy, historical accounts must necessarily lead out to the general history of society. Such an approach must lead away from the specific and historically bounded contexts of institutional history into the broader economic, political, social and cultural history. (Hake, 2010: 96)

The educational past might appear to be rather intellectual or academic, as opposed to being engaged in the battlefields of history where real blood is spilt... Yet the history of education is all about struggle. Education is at the heart of all the key struggles of modern times in different parts of the world. (McCulloch, 2011: 1)

Introduction

This chapter presents an overview of the changing landscape in adult education and lifelong learning. It discusses the role of UNESCO (the United Nations Educational Scientific and Cultural Organisation) in influencing policy discourses in recent years (Field, 2000; Tobias, 2004; Jarvis, 2011; Ouane, 2011; Rivera, 2011; Schuller, 2011; Milana, 2012). In addition, it touches on the contribution of the OECD (Organisation for Economic Co-operation and Development), the European Union and the World Bank in shifting the international focus from broadly based adult education for a range of purposes to lifelong learning for more narrowly economic ends. I first briefly sketch the various socio-political and economic shifts which have influenced conceptions of the purpose of adult education. For good or ill, the global discourse of lifelong learning, and the uses to which the term has been put, has crucially influenced adult education in the past 30 years. I therefore draw on the literature of international lifelong learning policy development and discuss its impact on adult education practice globally, before moving on in Chapter Two to discuss the development and current state of adult education in the two case study countries – England and Aotearoa New Zealand – which are the focus of this book.

The importance of history in understanding contemporary adult education

There are a number of ways in which a reader can understand the history of adult education (Hake, 2010). It has been related in the biographies of 'pioneering' individuals, such as Albert Mansbridge, Basil Yeaxlee, R. H. Tawney, John Dewey, Raymond Williams and Paulo Freire (Jarvis, 1987; McIlroy and Westwood, 1993; Coben, 1998; Mayo, 1999). But, as is evident from this roll-call, a history of individuals tends to be a history of (mainly middle class and white) men who came to enjoy power or influence and whose stories therefore have been extensively documented (Purvis, 1989). Only relatively recently, for example, has the leadership role of women, particularly in socialist adult education, been rescued from obscurity and their stories recounted (Martin, 2010). This history has also been told through literature documenting the work of prominent organisations such as the Mechanics Institutes, University Settlements, the university extension movement and the Workers' Educational Association (Hudson, 1851; Pimlott, 1935; Allaway, 1961; Marriott, 1991, 1998; Roberts, 2003) which have been important in the development of the organised practice of adult education in the English-speaking world. However, such accounts omit the influence of the indigenous communities and small, self-organised and sometimes 'underground' movements and groups which have played an important role in contesting dominant and elite notions of adult education (Hake, 2010). There have been many histories, too, written on adult education in specific countries of the English-speaking world (Thompson, 1945; Knowles, 1962; Kelly, 1970; Harrison, 1994; Tobias, 1994; Fieldhouse,

1996; Bowl and Tobias, 2012). These add to our understanding but perhaps may not offer a full sense of the influences on adult education which have crossed international boundaries and the social and political threads which bind practice in countries that are geographically separate. So below I trace the history of adult education through a chronology of key social and political influences.

Adult education has developed in the context of diverse, and sometimes conflicting, social and political ideas. Different historical periods have given rise to attempts on the part of those with power to control and direct access to knowledge and understanding. At the same time, these attempts have been contested by those who have been subject to them. Educational movements based in resistance and struggles for self-determination have therefore also arisen. A historical perspective on adult education deepens one's understanding of its diverse ideological antecedents and how these are echoed in current philosophy, policy and practice. It reveals the extent to which contemporary concerns have their roots in the past and the points at which major shifts in policy or practice took hold. It helps us to see that the present is a product of struggles, over time, between differing views and people in different power relationships (McCulloch, 2011). Most importantly perhaps, it enables us to see that the future can be changed through the actions of people and organisations. This chapter does not attempt to go over the historical ground in detail, but rather to provide an overview of the ways in which adult education practice has been influenced by the global spread of ideas.

Historical developments in adult education

Our understanding of the complexity of human settlement and achievement in prehistoric times enables us to recognise that more or less formalised learning activities must have been undertaken in the past in many parts of the world, though they would not, of course, have been labelled as such (Merriam and Brockett, 1997; Tobias, 2004). Rubenson (2010), in his overview of adult education, points out that in Egypt, China, India and the Greek and Roman empires adult education and training accompanied technological advances and the development of administrative systems which characterised previous civilisations. Adults have been engaged in forms of education and training for a range of purposes from the earliest times and across the world.

Recognition of the notion of adult education as *formalised provision* is a relatively recent phenomenon. It arose from processes of religious and cultural change, urbanisation, industrialisation and scientific advance as well as colonial expansion – and the struggles against it – beginning in Europe in the mid-sixteenth century and moving with increased rapidity during the late eighteenth and nineteenth centuries (Field, 2000:15; Hake, 2010). This period of massive social change had an impact on the field of adult education, whose development was driven by overlapping – and sometimes divergent – purposes and processes. In the twentieth century the provision of formalised adult education was influenced by liberal, humanist and socialist ideas and the intervention of the state in social affairs, while its philosophy was also influenced by the educational dimensions of anti- and post-colonial struggles. However, particularly since the early 1980s, globalisation of capitalism has intensified and the discourse of lifelong learning has been implicated in the transmission of neoliberal ideas to the adult education sector. Hake (2010) outlines some of the key historical periods of change which have had an impact on adult education in the United Kingdom, North America, Australia and New Zealand and are therefore of relevance to this book. Following Hake's model, I outline each below.

The Protestant Reformation

From the mid-sixteenth to mid-seventeenth centuries, during the period of Protestant Reformation in Northern and Central Europe, the growth of early forms of adult education was aided by the invention of the printing press and the translation of the Bible into the vernacular. Bible study groups fostered the dissemination of moral and religious ideas to adults by means of the written word – and led to an increase in literacy levels. This in turn stimulated demand for books of other kinds and the initiation of libraries and outlets for book sales. These developments mark the beginning of the idea of adult group learning and of the thirst for learning in groups, beyond the social elite.

The 'Enlightenment' and the French Revolution

The period of the late seventeenth and early eighteenth centuries, popularly known as the 'Age of Enlightenment', resulted in the spread of educational systems throughout Europe, as well as further rapid increases in literacy among men and, to a lesser extent, women, and the growth of a reading public. Ideas influenced by developments in scientific understanding began to challenge those based in a largely religious world view. Clubs, coffee houses and libraries developed as focal points for the discussion of politics, science and philosophy and thus became centres for informal and voluntary adult education, if not for all, then within a wider section of European public life than hitherto. The period of the French Revolution and, in particular, the 1789 *Declaration of the Rights of Man and of the Citizen* also gave stimulus to debate and organisation throughout Europe and beyond around ideas of civil equality and the right to education.

Colonial expansion

Also beginning in the mid-eighteenth century and gathering pace from the mid-nineteenth century, colonialism's influence on education was characterised by the export of Eurocentric ideas not only for the purpose of establishing and maintaining political, social, religious and cultural hegemony, but also to maintain morale and social control among settler populations. In the English-speaking colonial world this process saw the spread of moral and religious organisations, such as the missionary and temperance movements, and institutionalised education such as that later found in university extra mural and continuing education departments. The radical political consciousness generated by the French Revolution spread throughout Europe. By the beginning of the twentieth century in the United Kingdom and its colonies in Canada, Australia and New Zealand, self-organised adult education flourished alongside that offered by religious groups, trades unions and philanthropic movements.

Urbanisation and industrialisation

From the late eighteenth century through to the early 1930s the processes of industrialisation which began in the UK brought about major changes which influenced the development of formalised adult education. Technological advances and the intensification of industrial production signalled the need for training for a more skilled workforce – to which employers responded. The growth of urbanisation, which accompanied industrialisation, ushered in concern for the realisation of civic rights and the performance of civic duties. Adult educational organisations (such as Mechanics' Institutes and the Workers' Educational Association and the university extension movement) were established in the late part of the nineteenth and early twentieth centuries and were exported to Australia, New Zealand, Canada, the United States of America and elsewhere. The growing organisation of the working classes, the struggle for women's rights and the revolutionary climates in Europe and North America also gave rise to a range of more radical organisations concerned with the education of adults which were distinct from those inaugurated by the middle and upper classes.

The period after the 1914 to 1918 war in Europe stimulated a ferment of social and political movements, of the left and the right, in which the contestation of ideas – and thus the political and social education of adults – played an important part. Of particular significance in contemporary discussion of adult education is the work and writing of Antonio Gramsci in the period between 1926 and 1937 (Gramsci, 1971; Coben, 1998; Mayo, 1999). Gramsci's discussion of *hegemony*, the concept of *organic intellectuals* and of the distinction between *good sense* and *common sense* are central to contemporary radical socialist ideas of the role and purpose of adult education and the adult educator. This post-war period marked concerns about international solidarity and peaceful coexistence. It also saw the first attempt to link adult education organisations and movements internationally, by means of the 'World Association' for adult education (Fieldhouse, 1996).

A post-World War Two consensus on education

By the end of the Second World War in 1945 and until the late 1970s, humanistic notions of adult education supported the idea of education for a variety of purposes as a right for individuals as citizens. During this period and in a number of countries, the state assumed most responsibility for the education and training of adults. There was a growth in both adult education provision for non-vocational ends and support for community-based education activities. At the same time the notion of lifelong education began to be promoted – an idea that was taken up by UNESCO as early as 1949 (UNESCO, 2009) but most notably in the early to mid 1970s (Lengrand, 1970; Faure, 1972; Dave, 1976). Implicit in the humanistic perspective was a critique of conventional teaching methods and the introduction of the concept of the 'facilitation' of adults' learning (Rogers, 1969; Knowles, 1973).

Anti- and post-colonialism

The post-World War Two struggles against colonialism strongly influenced the philosophy and practice of adult education worldwide. Here the focus was on self-determination, nation building and social and political development in the context of struggles for liberation from colonial rule – particularly in Africa, Asia and South and Central America. In this way, the post-colonial movements of the 1960s and 1970s have been influential well beyond the decolonising world. Supported by a strong literature base (Freire, 1972; Illich, 1973; Nyerere, 1976), post-colonial educational ideas informed feminist, anti-war, anti-racist and anti-imperialist struggles across the globe and gave rise to the idea of consciousness-raising education as a condition for radical social change.

Globalising capitalism and neoliberalisation

Beginning in the United States and the United Kingdom, the period since the late 1970s has been characterised by the global spread of neoliberal ideologies and their application to the policy sphere. The dominance of neoliberalism has eclipsed the post-war humanist consensus and the radicalism of the 1960s and 1970s and has had far-reaching consequences for the structuring of publicly-funded provision and the organisation of education. It has involved the withdrawal of the state from areas of educational provision formerly regarded as being in the public domain and signalled a shift in post-compulsory education policy from the provision of education for a range of individual, social and vocational purposes to a narrower conception of education and training for primarily instrumental ends. Training for work and the need to accrue qualifications in the service of the 'knowledge economy' and international economic competitiveness is now the central focus of education policy in countries across the world. This shift has had major consequences for adult education practitioners, their perspectives on their work and their job prospects. Ironically, the liberal humanistic concept of lifelong learning has been harnessed to the service of this new economistic world view.

The global discourse of lifelong learning

Although the origins of the term 'lifelong education' (later re-dubbed lifelong learning) pre-date the post-World War Two era (Lindeman, 1926; Yeaxlee, 1929), the concept entered the mainstream of policy discourse in the early 1970s under the auspices of UNESCO (Field, 2000; Jarvis, 2011). Its emergence was prompted by a range of political, social and economic factors, well summarised as:

> *… the continuation of 'the cold war' and the ever increasing expenditure on defence and deployment of nuclear weapons, the rapid process of political de-colonization in Africa, Asia and the Pacific, and the continuing 'booms and busts' of a relatively slowly expanding global capitalist system. In addition they included the rise of 'new social movements' such as environmental, peace, indigenous peoples' and women's movements that raised increasingly questions about the Euro-centred and gendered nature of much of society and about the possibility of solving problems of wealth, poverty, peace and war, or of achieving sustainability of the eco-system within existing political and economic settlements.* (Tobias, 2004: 570)

Important, too, was an increasing recognition of the limitations of formal school-based and youth-focused education (Tobias, 2004; Jarvis, 2011). One of UNESCO's aims, expressed in two key UNESCO-commissioned reports published in the early 1970s (Lengrand, 1970; Faure, 1972), was to encourage governments to move away from an exclusive focus on expanding formal schooling and towards promoting education throughout the lifespan and in non-formal settings. All this might well have been an encouragement to adult educators to believe that an era of expanded adult education opportunities was heralded. However, as Jarvis (2011: 16) suggests, any optimism that adult educators may have entertained at this time is likely to have been dissipated by the way the international discourse of lifelong learning developed subsequently.

For the other players in the international policy field – the OECD, the World Bank and the European Union – economic concerns dominated the adult education agenda. While each of these organisations has a remit beyond economic development in terms of social and cultural integration and inclusion, education and training for work and international competitiveness has nevertheless trumped social aims. The OECD's remit includes the elimination of social disadvantage as well as employment and economic development. However, the focus of its contribution to policy development in the 1970s (OECD, 1973) became *recurrent education* as an answer to rising unemployment and rapid technological change (Rubenson, 2011). The capture of lifelong education for economic policy purposes began as long ago as the mid-1970s, but has intensified over the following decades, most notably in the 1990s (Delors, 1996; OECD, 1996; CEC, 2007). Field (2000) discusses this period in detail, drawing attention to the importance of the European Union in confirming lifelong learning as a central feature in education and labour market policies across the wider industrialised world.

Field (2000), Milana (2012) and contributors to Jarvis (2011) draw on the various policy documents produced by the OECD (see Schuller, 2011), UNESCO (see Ouane, 2011), the European Union (see Jarvis, 2011; Milana, 2012) and the World Bank (see Rivera, 2011) to trace:

> ... *the shift from adult education to lifelong learning that political globalization processes have favoured.* (Milana, 2012:104)

This shift in language from *adult education* via *lifelong education* to *lifelong learning,* which is apparent in international and national government pronouncements, concerns adult educators through its implications for adult education as a field of practice. It shows that policy expectations have shifted in three main ways:

- from social and individual to primarily economic objectives;
- from institutional to individual responsibility for ensuring participation;
- from education as public good to education as a market commodity.

By means of this shift, now widely reflected in national as well as international policies, adult education has been reconstructed to focus on training for work and away from individual and social development. Furthermore, the adult educator has been pushed from centre stage as the learner is now deemed responsible for directing, planning – and paying for – his/her own learning.

The capture of adult education for lifelong learning policy hegemony

> *By bringing the agency of the learner to the foreground, public policy shades off the agency of the educator engaged in teaching-learning transactions or broader educative relations, while interfering with the politics of everyday life.* (Milana, 2012: 105)

Across the world, the policy consensus in favour of lifelong learning and adult education for primarily economic ends is now almost unanimous. Governments have borrowed from each other, adapting policies on education and training to their national contexts. The impact of this is that paid employment opportunities for adult educators have been increasingly restricted to training for, or in, work and to credentialised learning. That is not to say that there has been no emphasis at all on education for social inclusion and social cohesion. However, when it comes to the distribution of resources, the low priority placed on non-work related education is clearly apparent (Field, 2000).

The dominance of lifelong learning as a policy discourse raises other problems. As Field (2000: 102) suggests, lifelong learning may not only be guilty of narrowing the possibilities for education, it may also be reproducing inequality through its tendency to emphasise the exclusion of those who have had least access to education. In a situation of increasing unemployment, coupled with credential inflation (Dore, 1997), those without qualifications, in particular those with lower literacy levels, are the least likely to have access to jobs and to meaningful educational opportunities. The promotion of lifelong learning as an individual responsibility and a panacea for the ills of economy and society has re-cast education increasingly as a compulsory activity on which social acceptance, career advancement or state support may depend (Coffield, 1999). The impact for adult educators is the transformation of their role from the facilitation of willing learners to the management of the successful course completion of educational conscripts.

A further and more subtle aspect of the impact of neoliberalism on adult education has been discussed by Martin (2001, 2005). He argues that the deconstruction of welfare has been predicated on a reconstruction of the notion of citizenship, which in much adult education work is now defined in terms of individuals' responsibility to accept and assume their place in the economic world order. Citizenship education – once a forum for facilitating critical debate and social action – has consequently, Martin suggests, become a vehicle for domestication rather than liberation:

> *As the state's role shifts from doing things to enabling them to happen, from intervention to facilitation (i.e. managing the contexts in which citizens make their own autonomous choices) so it is*

necessary to prepare such 'empowered' citizens for their unaccustomed civic self-sufficiency. (Martin, 2005: 575)

Adult educators engaged in active citizenship education, social skills training, English for Speakers of Other Languages (ESOL) teaching and Personal and Community Development Learning are implicated in a process through which the term 'empowerment' has taken on a very different meaning from that proposed by their radical forebears of the 1960s and 1970s (Coare and Johnson, 2003; Fryer, 2010). As Martin argues, empowerment – defined as the development of political awareness as a precursor to social action which is, in turn, directed to the creation of a more socially just and equal social order – has been denuded of its radical meaning. In its place the neoliberalised notion of 'empowerment' signifies self-efficacy, self-sufficiency and personal responsibility for ensuring one's own economic and personal well-being.

Adult education in the current context

Everywhere in the world statements identify adult education as a key to the survival of humankind in the 21st century, attributing adult education with the magic to contribute positively to education for all… and yet, almost everywhere in the world, adult education is a widely neglected and feeble part of the official education scene. (UNESCO 1997: 3–4)

In the foreword to its *Global Report on Adult Education and Lifelong Learning*, UNESCO (2009: 8) refers to its own 'pioneering role in affirming the critical role of adult education in the development of society and promoting a comprehensive approach to learning through-out life'. This gives a flavour of the breadth of the vision of lifelong learning as originally laid out. However, while the internationalisation of the concept of lifelong education may have been spearheaded internationally by UNESCO, its vision has been eclipsed by policy scripts of other, more economically-focused ideological forces, agencies and governments. UNESCO itself acknowledges the primacy of vocational training, at the expense of other forms of education in the wealthier countries (including England and New Zealand). It notes the increasing marketisation and privatisation of adult education in these countries. It describes some of the features which now characterise adult education across a range of countries:

- the restriction of public provision to minimum purposes and the lowest levels;
- the tendency for adult education beyond 'the minimum' to be given over to commercial providers or non-government agencies whose provision is reliant on market forces;
- the instability of provision as a result of the unpredictability of funding;
- a consequent weakening of governance structures for the provision of adult education;
- the threat to equity as a result of the increasing dominance of the profit motive in adult education provision.

In summary, it states:

> *The fluctuation and instability of public funds for adult education further underscores the sensitivity and vulnerability of this sector. With an unstable legal and financial framework, adult education provision is extremely susceptible to even minor economic or political change.* (UNESCO, 2009: 56)

Even from the perspective of UNESCO, which could hardly be described as an over-critical organisation, the prospects for a publicly provided adult education system which pays attention to issues of equality and social justice do not appear good.

Summary

This chapter has outlined some of the ideas and events in history which have influenced the development of adult education globally as a field characterised by diversity and contested philosophical and political views. It has described how the dominance of neoliberalism has overshadowed radical and liberal/humanist ideas, has swept away policy and funding support for adult education – which is not geared to economic aims – and has left provision for non-instrumental ends to be offered in the educational marketplace. It has discussed how the discourse of lifelong learning has been captured in support of neoliberal aims, re-casting education and training in the richer industrialised countries as an individual responsibility. The next chapter looks in more detail at the influence of the global and the local on adult education in two such countries – England and New Zealand.

CHAPTER TWO

England and New Zealand:
Two national contexts for adult education

Apart from some common traditions, there are marked and startling similarities both in the rhetoric of reform and in the distance travelled towards the entrenchment of neoliberal policies. Despite the implementation of neoliberal education policies in other countries, there are few places where reform has proceeded with such similarity of pace, approach, rhetoric and policy patterns. (Gordon and Whitty, 1997: 454)

Introduction

This chapter describes the development and current context for adult education in two case study countries – England and Aotearoa New Zealand. Although separated by a distance of over 12,000 miles, and marked by geographical, demographic and cultural differences, England and New Zealand share aspects of a common heritage as a result of migration, colonisation and the continuing flow of people and ideas between the two countries (Bowl and Tobias, 2012). They also share more recent experience of the zealous application of neoliberal ideas to all aspects of education (Gordon and Whitty, 1997), including post-compulsory education. While the impact of neoliberalism has been powerful in both countries, the specifics of demography, history and culture may also shape the possibilities for action suggesting differences as well as convergences in education policy and practice (McLean, 1992; Phillips and Schweisfurth, 2008). The chapter begins with a description of the demographic and historical contexts for adult education in both countries. It then goes on to discuss the development of policy around adult and community education in recent times and considers how policy changes are being played out in practice.

New Zealand and England: A brief demographic sketch

The majority of Aotearoa New Zealand's population of just over four million resides in 16 urban centres on New Zealand's North or South Islands, with over half the population located in six cities: Auckland, Christchurch, Dunedin, Hamilton, Tauranga and Wellington (the capital). Away from these urban centres, New Zealand is sparsely populated and largely rural. This relatively small population enables social networks to flourish, in spite of geographical differences. Its economy is based on agriculture, tourism and small to medium-sized industries. Māori, the earliest inhabitants, make up just under 15 per cent of the population; people of European (Pākehā) heritage make up the majority at around 70 per cent. New Zealand's ethnic make-up is increasingly diverse, however, and people of Pacific Island (Pasifika) and East Asian heritage make up sizeable minorities. New Zealand today is officially a bicultural and bilingual state in which Māori, Pākehā and new migrants from across the globe coexist within the context of the Treaty of Waitangi (Ministry of Education, 2008; Statistics New Zealand, 2013).*

In the United Kingdom in recent years the devolution of many government functions (including education) to its constituent countries – England, Northern Ireland, Scotland and Wales – has led to a divergence in adult education policies. England is the most highly populated of the four countries of the United Kingdom. Its population (around 53 million) is much larger than that of New Zealand. Like New Zealand, it is ethnically diverse. According to the ethnic classifications of the United Kingdom's Office for National Statistics (2012) the population includes around 80 per cent white British inhabitants with minority populations

---

* The Treaty of Waitangi, signed in 1840 by representatives of the British Government and a number of chiefs of Māori tribes, established British governorship in Aotearoa New Zealand, whilst also recognizing, inter alia, Māori rights to land and property ownership. Today, the Treaty is an important document which underpins the bicultural status of Aotearoa New Zealand and relationships between Māori and Pākehā (those of European settler heritage).

of South Asian, African Caribbean and African heritage (totalling around 11 per cent) and other ethnic backgrounds, including European and East Asian. Compared with New Zealand, England is highly urbanised as a consequence of its industrial past. Heavy industry has been in decline for a number of years; the country's economy is now based on a mix which includes manufacturing, chemical and pharmaceutical, finance, service and agricultural industries. At the time of writing, England's unemployment rate, at 7.8 per cent, was higher than that of New Zealand (6.8 per cent).

Two historical contexts for adult education

A number of writers (Walker, 1990; King, 2003; Tobias, 1994, 2004) have explored the pre-colonial and pre-capitalist history of education in New Zealand. Prior to European settlement, Māori kinship-based social and organisational arrangements were central to the passing on of knowledge, understanding and skills within and across generations. While European settlement from the 1700s initially resulted in a two-way flow of knowledge between indigenous and newcomer populations, the incorporation of New Zealand into the British colonial political economy in the nineteenth century established a new hegemony (Walker, 1990). The development of educational institutions on a British model was integral to colonial strategies for extending British influence. Today, adult and community education (ACE) largely reflects this colonial past. But colonisation and its impact did not go uncontested; the current structure and discourse of ACE in New Zealand also reflect the 'military, political, economic and ideological' struggles (Tobias, 2004: 570) of and between Māori and Pākehā (Tobias, 2004; Bowl and Tobias, 2012). A key moment in those struggles was the signing of the Treaty of Waitangi in 1840 which officially established a formal partnership between the country's indigenous people and its colonial settlers. However, it did not put an end to the appropriation of Māori land, or to the suppression of Māori language, culture and ways of knowing – which Māori continued to resist. Nevertheless the Treaty of Waitangi still defines the relationship between Māori and non-Māori within the parameters of a bicultural state in which the values, language and world view of both should be respected.

In England, prior to industrialisation, adult education and learning were largely informally organised and religious and vocational in nature.

32

Formally organised adult education arose in the wake of nineteenth century industrial and imperial expansion, urbanisation, technological advance and, crucially, the growth of an organised working class (Williams, 1961a, 1961b; Simon, 1965, 1990; Thompson, 1980; Fieldhouse, 1996; Field, 2000). It was driven by a number of sometimes complementary and sometimes contradictory motives. First, the explosion in scientific and technical knowledge was accompanied by a growing interest on the part of working- and middle-class people to understand the many developments which were affecting their lives. Second, there was a desire on the part of some employers for a more skilled workforce to facilitate capitalist competition with an industrialising Europe and North America. Third, there was concern among liberal elites, municipal authorities and central government about how to manage some of the problems arising from urbanisation, including poor economic and social conditions and the social unrest which accompanied these. Fourth, as working people became more self-organised there was a growth in autonomous educational associations, often linked to radical or socialist political aspirations (Simon, 1965, 1990; Fieldhouse, 1996). From its early origins, therefore, adult education in England was driven by diverse aims – instrumental, liberal and radical – and organised by diverse actors – industrialists, religious organisations and workers – either separately or in alliance.

Many of the educational organisations formed in the UK during the nineteenth century were short-lived and localised. However some, like the Mechanics' Institutes and the university extension movement, persisted into the twentieth century. Fieldhouse (1996) provides a detailed history of the development of these organisations in the UK. He describes the impetus behind Mechanics' Institutes as being: 'A mixture of autonomous working-class enterprise and paternalistic middle-class provision' (ibid. 23) whose classes on topics of scientific and cultural interests were directed primarily towards skilled working- and lower middle-class men, rather than the unemployed or unskilled worker. The WEA, which was formed in 1903, linked organised labour and the universities and aimed to provide manual labourers with access to university education and knowledge (Roberts, 2003). Again, however, it was an alliance between middle class liberal intellectuals and working class organisations, rather than an independent workers' movement. In addition, the focus of these organisations was primarily, though not exclusively, male (Purvis, 1989; Martin, 2010). Although adult education initiatives tended to focus on men, and although women tended to be excluded from higher level education, this is not to say that women were not active in their own right. Jane Martin (2010) for example, describes the life and work of Mary Bridges Adams, one of the female campaigners for working-class education whose contribution has been neglected, while Robert Tobias (1994) describes the various female-led organisations which grew up in New Zealand, among whose aims were the extension of educational opportunities to women.

These organisations, along with libraries for working men and Christian and temperance organisations, were among those imported from Britain to New Zealand in the late nineteenth and early twentieth centuries to cater for the needs of European migrants and to regulate male settler social life. As in England, the motivations for their importation were diverse, but included social control as well as educational emancipation. The Mechanics' Institutes (Hudson, 1851; Sims, 2010) were relatively short lived but, in New Zealand as well as in England, the WEA has continued to provide adult education opportunities. The nature of these opportunities has varied from place to place, depending on the local context and funding available. In New Zealand the focus has been on political and cultural education. In England in recent years WEA provision has increasingly been tied in with accreditation and government funding priorities. In both countries the tension between middle class and working class interests has been a feature of the internal debates of these organisations (Simon, 1990; Tobias, 1994; Fieldhouse, 1996).

One of the debates in the struggles for working class and radical education, which remains relevant today (CCCS, 1981), centres on the extent to which popular adult education should be developed independently of state and philanthropic intervention (substitutional strategies) and the extent to which the efforts of those advocating for adult education should be directed towards securing publicly funded provision (statist strategies). Linked to this has been the debate around the forms of knowledge and understanding which should be fostered. In this context, 'Really Useful Knowledge' – practical political knowledge of the economy, social sciences and politics which provides adults with the means to understand and change society (Johnson, 1979), was advocated, in opposition to 'merely' useful knowledge, which was seen as being imposed by middle class interests in an attempt to neutralise self-organised and more politically challenging working class adult educational projects. These debates are echoed in contemporary struggles over the funding and purposes of adult education (Mayo and Thompson, 1995; Thompson, 1997; Foley, 1999).

The early history of adult education in England and New Zealand demonstrates the way in which industrialisation and colonial expansion aided the development and dissemination of adult educational ideas and organisations. This aspect of their shared history has led to some continuity between the two countries' adult education traditions which reflect a mix of motivations – conservative, liberal, humanist and radical. However, in New Zealand the influence of Māori culture, language and organisation is significant and the struggles of Māori to challenge hegemonic educational ideas and structures (Walker, 1990) have been and remain important in claiming and maintaining space in New Zealand for education with social and cultural aims.

Adult and community education and the rise of the Welfare State

Throughout the nineteenth century in both England and New Zealand the state's role in adult education was negligible. However, in spite of economic booms and busts and the losses and disruptions caused by two World Wars, the first half of the twentieth century was marked by increased state interest in the education of adults. In England, the 1902 Education Act saw the creation of Local Education Authorities which became responsible for adult education, as well as elementary and some secondary education (Fieldhouse, 1996). Similarly, in New Zealand, state subsidies began to be made available for the provision of technical and other forms of adult education (Tobias, 1994), though equivalent local government structures were not developed to administer and fund education, and this remains the case (Gordon and Whitty, 1997).

In England after the 1914–1918 World War there was high level support for the idea of adult education becoming available to the mass of the people. The argument was made for adult education's social purpose and its contribution to building and sustaining participatory democracy. This support was expressed through the Smith Report (Ministry of Reconstruction, 1919) which was commissioned by the UK government as part of its planning for post-war reconstruction. Local education authorities and some of the larger voluntary organisations (including the WEA and universities) were designated as 'responsible bodies' in respect of adult education and charged with providing both long and shorter courses of non-accredited adult education from 1924. This set the pattern for funding for many years to come – a mix of local and central government subsidy to public and voluntary bodies working independently of one another. Through and between both World Wars, adult education in England continued to survive, addressing a range of purposes, reflecting the perceived needs of the times but subject to the vicissitudes of the economic climate.

A similar picture was discernible in New Zealand. For example, the depression of the early 1930s saw widespread cuts in state expenditure on public services including adult education. However, as Tobias (1994) points out, even in periods of economic stringency independent popular study groups continued to thrive in New Zealand as working people engaged in political action and debate. As the national economy began to recover, and with the election of a Labour Government in 1935, funding was restored to some organisations and new adult and community education initiatives also began to spring up. The 1938 Education Amendment Act led to the establishment of a centralised National Council for Adult Education which assumed responsibility for advising on adult education and distributing funds to adult education organisations. At the same time, in the late 1930s and early 1940s a number of Young Māori Leaders' Conferences were held which debated issues faced by Māori, especially in view of rapid urbanisation (Thompson, 1945; Walker, 1990; Tobias, 1994; Bowl and Tobias, 2012). These conferences reflected the continuing struggle for self-determination and for a future for Māori which went beyond the Labour government's aspiration for socio-economic equalisation in the context of the Welfare State. In addition, they encompassed struggles in relation to education, language and culture which continue to be reflected in debates around adult education policy (Hill, 2004).

While the engagement of England and New Zealand in the Second World War diverted resources and political attention away from educational developments in the civilian realm, adult education activity was sustained (Tobias, 1994; Fieldhouse, 1996). Furthermore, educational provision for those serving in the armed forces was established in both countries from the early 1940s. Its purposes were diverse and embraced general interest education, preparation for re-entry into civilian life and citizenship and social and political education. The latter was sometimes seen as controversial, however, particularly when it was offered by non-

Forces organisations and, as Fieldhouse reports in relation to England, it rarely went uncensored.

As World War Two drew to a close in England, the 1944 Education Act heralded the introduction of more egalitarian principles to the educational sphere. Among the Act's provisions was support for post-compulsory education for a range of purposes including cultural enrichment and recreation (Fieldhouse, 1996) and part-time continuing education for young workers (Tinkler, 2001). Local Education Authorities were charged with providing full- and part-time post-compulsory educational opportunities, in consultation with other providers, including local universities and voluntary bodies. Evening classes and university extra-mural provision expanded. But a plan by the Ministry of Education to develop further education colleges as the hub for vocational and non-vocational adult education throughout the country, supported by networks of more localised centres, did not materialise due to a combination of lack of political will and lack of finance. As a result, further education colleges focused primarily on vocational training, while local education authority evening institutes, community centres and voluntary sector organisations focused on non-vocational adult education, reinforcing a tacit demarcation between adult (non-vocational) and further (vocational) education which, as Fieldhouse suggests, had already been mooted by the 1919 Smith Report. The key post-war development in New Zealand adult education was the 1947 Adult Education Act which established the National Council of Adult Education, along with regional councils (based in the universities). During this period too, schools-based adult education expanded considerably and, until relatively recently, schools remained the major providers of non-vocational, non-accredited adult education for local individuals and communities.

The development of the Welfare State in both countries brought with it a measure of expansion in community-based adult education, and laid the funding foundations for some of the institutions which have hosted adult and community education activity from then to the present day. However the main educational focus was secondary schooling. Although there were plans in both countries for more comprehensive development of a system of adult education these rarely came to full fruition, but were limited by lack of investment and uneven political will. Also discernible in both countries is the ongoing tension around the purposes of adult education, the extent to which it should be socially and politically engaged and the division between vocational and non-vocational purposes (Williams, 1961a).

The sixties and seventies: Radical influences and educational idealism

The processes of decolonisation stimulated radical thinking worldwide (Freire, 1972; Illich, 1973; Nyerere, 1976) and ushered in a period of optimism about possibilities for adult education. The May 1968 uprisings of students and workers in France also brought to the fore issues around the relationship between intellectuals and the workers movement. Moreover, global social movements – anti-apartheid, anti-nuclear, environmentalist, indigenous and feminist – gave practical meaning to learning through struggle outside state funding and control.

At the same time, growing international interest in lifelong education sponsored through UNESCO and the OECD (Lengrand, 1970; Faure, 1972; Dave, 1976) provided a counterbalance to the historical emphasis on formal schooling. This, too, influenced adult educators' ideas about the possibilities of non-formal approaches to education (Tobias, 2004; Jarvis, 2011). As discussed in Chapter One these developments were international in scale but also significant in their impact on national contexts for adult education. Radical political and educational ideas stimulated popular education movements; they also influenced publicly funded adult educators who were employed in the developing adult and community education field. In the early 1970s government policy also began to reflect a socially-oriented view of adult education's purpose.

In England radical ideas were influential in the work of adult and community educators appointed to the Inner London (ILEA) and other Local Education Authorities. The ILEA replaced the London County Council in 1965. It assumed responsibility for the network of adult education institutes which existed around London and which engaged in educational work with local communities, in literacy education and teaching English as a foreign language as well as in the provision of more traditional evening classes. While relationships between the young, radically-influenced (and usually part-time) adult education workers and the more bureaucratic outlook of Local Education Authorities was at times somewhat fraught, it was a period when, viewed in retrospect, a hundred adult and community education flowers seemed to bloom. In the policy arena, the Russell Committee was appointed to advise the government on policies for adult education. The consequent report (DES, 1973) supported the creation of a number of agencies to promote specific types of provision including the Adult Literacy Resources Agency and The National Institute for Adult Education (now NIACE) as well as supporting residential adult education. The intention behind the report was to lay out a plan for adult education within the context of a national education system and it appeared at the time to presage further development. The report recommended the expansion of non-vocational adult education as a vehicle for helping adults to adjust to rapidly changing times. However, this promise was never fully realised as economic crises and rising unemployment turned government attention increasingly towards vocational education and training and on preparing young people for work (Callaghan, 1976), rather than education for broader social purposes (Field, 2000). Humanistic ideals were overtaken by an instrumentalist policy approach which has virtually eradicated liberal humanistic policy discourses.

In New Zealand, under the 1972–1975 Labour administration adult and community education similarly gained momentum with the expansion of government-supported adult education for non-vocational and social ends which raised the status of adult education and heralded increased participation (Tobias, 2004). Among the initiatives funded by government and which employed adult and community educators were community colleges, adult literacy projects and rural education activities programmes (REAPs). From 1979, 13 REAPS were established with the aim of improving educational services across the board in rural areas. Community adult educators employed by REAPS, together with school-based adult education co-ordinators, became the bedrock of national organisations which represented the interests of adult education.

At the same time, and outside the confines of policy-driven adult education in New Zealand, many informal adult education activities accompanied various political movements – for peace, anti-nuclear armament and for women's and Māori rights (Locke, 1992). Walker (1990) points to the Māori renaissance from the late 1970s and the work of the Māori Women's Welfare League and Nga Tamatoa (the young warriors) in promoting the resurgence of Māori language. From the 1970s there was rapid growth in the teaching of Māori in schools and the community (Bowl and Tobias, 2012). A key moment in the recent history of political action in New Zealand was the 1981 South African Rugby tour of New Zealand which sparked a massive resistance movement and divided national opinion. Thousands of people were involved in protests wherever matches were held and Beyer (1981) describes some of the informal learning from such campaigns to demonstrate the power of popular education outside the control of the state. However, a crisis in capitalism, mounting unemployment and the growing influence of neoliberalising ideologies brought adult education expansion to a halt in both countries, and the late 1970s and early 1980s marked a retreat from the post-war welfare consensus which progressively impacted on adult education and which continues to the present.

Struggles with neoliberalism

Since the early 1980s both England and New Zealand have experienced the aggressive implementation of neoliberal policy which has had an impact on education across the board (Gordon and Whitty, 1997). The key features of this shift have been the pulling back of the state from large parts of the public sector, a diminution of concern with social relations and a reliance on the 'market' to deliver national economic prosperity. For adult and community education, whose position has been historically marginal and vulnerable, the impact has been particularly stark. While there have been some differences in pace and detail, 'user pays' and training for skills, employment and employability have become the policy mantra in both countries and there have been remarkable similarities in policy statements and funding priorities.

England and the legacy of Thatcherism
In England in the early 1980s, a Conservative government under the Prime Ministership of Margaret Thatcher asserted a strongly instrumentalist and individualised vision for education and training. This view persisted through the term of the Labour Government from 1997 to 2010, the administration's policy rhetoric around lifelong learning notwithstanding (DfEE, 1998), and into the present under a Conservative-led coalition. Adult educators' practice shifted increasingly towards training for employment. In addition, an element of compulsion was introduced into training for the unemployed. Of particular significance for adult educators' work was the government's attack on local authorities. The 1988 Education Reform Act reduced the power of, and hence the funding available to, local education authorities; the Inner London Education Authority was abolished and community-

based adult education was much diminished. Following this, the 1992 Further and Higher Education Act took further education colleges out of local authority control, establishing them as corporate bodies within a developing education market. Further education colleges were charged with responsibility for vocational education and training, basic skills, education for people with learning difficulties and access to higher education programmes. While further education expanded, adult and community education increasingly became residual. Local education authorities and the private and voluntary sector were left to manage personal and community development learning, with shrinking resources and shrinking policy support (Osborne and Sankey, 2009).

One area of adult education which did not decline during this period and which was enthusiastically embraced by further education colleges, local education authorities and some voluntary adult and community organisations was adult access to higher education provision (more commonly known as access courses). Access courses were an educational response to rising adult unemployment but also grew out of a movement among adult educators and others to open up routes to higher level educational opportunities, particularly for women and ethnic minorities who had earlier been excluded from these. Increasingly, however, access courses have become bound into formal accreditation and quality control systems and geared towards access to vocational study – nursing, health and social care being the most popular pathways (Quality Assurance Agency for Higher Education, 2011). As Benn and Burton (1995) have suggested, this has presented a dilemma for adult educators engaged in work, which began with a socially transformative purpose and has been reshaped to individual and instrumentalist ends.

Policies of instrumentalism, vocationalism and accreditation were further cemented by the implementation of the recommendations of the Leitch Review (2006). The Review's recommendations aimed to make the UK a world leader in skills as a means to enable it to compete in the global economy. Along with the White Paper *Further Education: Raising Skills, Improving Life Chances* (DfES, 2006), it established skills for work, minimum levels of accredited attainment and individuals' responsibility for investment in their own education and training as the dominant discourse for adult education. Despite the White Paper's acknowledgement of the desirability of an educational agenda that goes wider than skills training, the government was explicit about its intention not to fund it:

> *... there will increasingly be an expectation that individuals should pay for this kind of provision where they can afford to do so.* (DfES, 2006: 31)

A further development which has affected the flexibility and responsiveness of organised adult education has been the policy focus on 'quality' and 'standards' and 'outcomes' defined by government (LSC, 2000; Ofsted, 2013). Regimes of inspection now extend to all providers of adult education, from large further education colleges to community-based, voluntary and local authority organisations. At the same time, adult educators have been expected to meet minimum expectations in relation to their own qualifications and continuing professional development (DfES, 2004); from 2007 until 2012 all entrants to adult education were required to gain qualified teacher status.

There has been limited resistance. NIACE (The National Institute of Adult Continuing Education) seeks to advocate on behalf of adult learners in England and Wales. However, its membership is relatively small (NIACE, 2010a), its advocacy role has been one of 'critical friendship' with government (NIACE, 2010b) and it is also a contractor of work for government which arguably compromises its ability to campaign against the impact of cuts in the sector. In 2008 the Campaigning Alliance for Lifelong Learning (CALL), a loose alliance of trade unions, student groups and adult education providers, came together to lobby for the maintenance of support for adult education for personal wellbeing and development as well as instrumental ends. More recently, Action for ESOL has mobilised learners, teachers and trade unions and has had some success in stemming the tide of cutbacks in educational provision for migrants and refugees. The advocacy and campaigning work of these organisations will be discussed in Chapter Eight. Overall, however, reduced subsidies, instrumentalist agendas, accreditation regimes and 'quality' controls have decimated English community-based adult education, while college-based adult education is tied into vocational training and certification, and universities have all but lost the fight for liberal adult education. The bulk of paid adult education work is now confined to literacy, ESOL and vocational training.

New Zealand and the neoliberal experiment

It has been argued (Tobias, 2004; Zepke, 2009) that 1987 marked the point at which policy in New Zealand – under a succession of governments, but beginning with a Labour government – became dominated by neoliberal ideas. The 1989 Education Act created the Tertiary Education Commission and, importantly for adult education, it ushered in open entry to tertiary education for adults over 20 years of age, regardless of their previous qualifications. Open access for mature students has been a unique but increasingly controversial aspect of education policy, particularly since 2009, as government has capped university numbers and penalised universities with low retention rates (Healy and Gunby, 2012). The 1989 Act (New Zealand Government, 1989) also formally recognised Wānanga – public tertiary institutions providing education in a specifically Māori cultural context (Walker, 1990). The 1990 Education Amendment Act saw the restructuring of post-compulsory education and established a largely demand-led framework for tertiary education which Tobias describes as a compromise between competing ideologies, with some resultant contradictions:

> *On the one hand, it went some way toward breaking down*
> *institutional barriers to learning and allowed for the possibility of*
> *a more diverse curriculum; on the other hand, it endorsed a highly*
> *individualized and consumerist notion of lifelong learning and a*
> *managerialist approach to problem solving. It appeared to allow little*
> *space for the development of radical or critical engagements based on the*
> *collective interests of groups and movements in society…* (2004: 576)

The election of a National Party government in 1990 was to further worsen the position of adult education (Benseman, 2005) and bring about drastic funding cuts and the removal of government advisory support which, in turn, precipitated a fall in membership of ACE Aotearoa (the national umbrella organisation) and a decline in morale and activity.

However, Tobias (2004) describes how some practitioners kept the vision of a progressive future alive through the 1990s with little state funding or recognition. Adult educators continued to organise nationally, while maintaining international engagement through UNESCO. Walker (1990) describes the activities of Māori organisations during this time, in particular the 1984 Māori Educational Development Conference and its radical influence in advancing Māori education. ACE Aotearoa national conferences featured speeches which contested the assumptions of neoliberalism and highlighted the radicalism of adult education manifested through struggles around Māori language education and culture and the Treaty of Waitangi. Although the history of ACE in New Zealand during the 1980s and 1990s may appear a story of defeat, there was some continuity of progressive thought and action informed by radical education ideas and traditions. The momentum of protest over economic and social policy changes grew through the late 1980s and early 1990s and contributed to a change in government and a degree of change in policy direction in 1999.

The 1999 Labour Alliance government (Codd, 2002; Zepke, 2009) pursued a Third Way (Giddens, 1998, 2000, 2001) in politics, seeking to reconcile neoliberal and social democratic ideologies and create a socialised market economy. For adult educators this brief period was one of increased optimism. The government established the Tertiary Education Advisory Commission (TEAC) which became the Tertiary Education Commission (TEC) in 2003. The TEC assumed responsibility for policy and funding in the whole post-compulsory education sector. This, in theory, gave ACE equal standing alongside polytechnics, universities, industrial training organisations and other educational organisations. The government acknowledged adult and community education as a public and private good and advocated a collaborative approach to rebuilding the ACE sector. An Adult Education and Community Learning Working Party was set up to consult with the ACE sector. The result of the working party's considerations was *Koia! Koia! Towards a Learning Society* (TEC, 2001) which defined ACE and outlined a vision for its future. The sector was charged with focusing on five priorities which reflected a range of aims – individual and social, compensatory and liberal:

- targeting learners whose initial learning was not successful
- raising foundation skills
- encouraging lifelong learning
- strengthening communities
- strengthening social cohesion.

Central to policy at this point was an understanding that the ACE sector should take 'ownership' of its defined role and accompanying responsibilities. The promise of funding was used as an incentive to encourage the sector to work collaboratively through regional networks to co-ordinate provision to meet local needs, and implement quality systems and professional development plans. Meanwhile Māori

44

and Pasifika organisations laid out their own ACE agenda based on self-determination, self-organisation and distinctive conceptions of knowledge, learning and teaching (K. Irwin, 2008; Morrison and Vaioleti, 2008). It seemed that the place of non-accredited education within tertiary education had been publicly recognised.

However, over time, the Labour coalition's interest in ACE appeared to wane and the global drive for education and training for the knowledge economy became more influential. This is reflected in the decreased prominence of ACE within the government's Tertiary Education Strategy (TEC, 2007) which devoted just six lines to ACE. Hopes for increased, secure and equitable funding were not realised and the government's aspirations to meet industry's needs through training, to link research to economic opportunities, and to improve workforce literacy and numeracy took precedence over funding for more general, community-based purposes.

A change of government and an economic downturn signalled renewed problems for ACE in New Zealand from the 2008 general election when the Labour-led coalition was replaced by a centre-right coalition led by the National Party. One of the new government's first acts was to cut staffing in the Tertiary Education Commission and funding for ACE. Funding to schools-based adult education was slashed and support for university- and polytechnic-based community education was phased out from 2011. General interest, non-accredited liberal education (characterised by the then Minister of Education as 'hobby classes') was the first to be targeted. School and university adult educators, along with community educators in REAPs, had been the main recipients of funded provision and therefore the most active in regional and national organisations representing adult and community education. Funding cutbacks resulted in the loss of many of these practitioners and thereby the capacity for organised opposition. The New Zealand government's Tertiary Education Strategy for 2010–2015 (TEC, 2010a) reveals the nature of the policy shift as the five priorities for ACE were replaced by three target groups and were clearly individual, compensatory and instrumental in tone:

- to serve learners whose first learning experience was unsuccessful
- to assist those seeking pathways into tertiary education
- to assist people who lack literacy, language and numeracy skills for work and further study.

The current government's view of the contribution of liberal education was clarified further in its guidance to ACE organisations:

> *Organisations are welcome to continue to deliver hobby and personal interest courses; however as these are not TEC funded please do not include them in your completed template.* (TEC, 2010b)

The fragile certainties of the previous ten years were rapidly undermined and although a spirited defence was mounted against the cuts (Fordyce and Papa, 2009; Tully, 2009) it did not prevent their implementation.

2013: Where are the adult and community educators?

In the past five years there have been, in both countries, further reductions in publicly funded adult education provision and jobs. Those who remain in employment are likely to have experienced job insecurity and reductions in classes taught and hours of work. The move towards marketisation has shifted some adult educators towards the private sector and others out of employment.

In England, the decline in adult education has been unrelenting since the election of Margaret Thatcher's Conservative government in 1979. There was no revival under the 1997–2010 Labour governments such as was seen in New Zealand under a Labour-led coalition from 1999–2008. While in New Zealand non-accredited education is still a feature of the ACE landscape, adult education practitioners in both countries are now subject to more targeted, competitive approaches and tighter accountability regimes. The post-war welfare consensus which countenanced the funding of adult education for a broad range of purposes has been all but swept away. State-funded adult education is increasingly confined to a narrow range of purposes. Nevertheless, adult educators in both countries, whether paid or unpaid, continue to practice in diverse contexts across the public, voluntary and private sectors. The implications of these changes for their work and how they view their purposes, their practice and their prospects in the current policy climate will be explored in Section Two.

Table 2.1 Where are the adult and community educators?

England	New Zealand
• University continuing education departments	• University continuing education departments
• Further education and sixth form colleges	• Wānanga
• Local education authorities and other public sector organisations	• Polytechnics/technical institutions
• Local education authorities and other public sector organisations	• Schools
• National and local non-profit organisations	• Rural Education Activities Providers
• Work-based training organisations	• Iwi-based (Māori tribal) groups
• Trade unions	• National and local non-profit organisations
• Penal institutions	• Work-based training organisations
• Private training providers	• Penal institutions
• Informal organisations and campaigning groups	• Private training providers
	• Informal organisations and campaigning groups

Summary

This chapter has described the history and development of adult education in England and New Zealand. Historically, the influence of British colonialism on adult education in New Zealand has been substantial. Many of the adult education activities and organisations which exist there today reflect the past and continuing relationship between the two countries. More recently, neoliberalising policies have had a forceful impact on both countries and, as a result, adult educators in England and New Zealand face similar questions around the purposes of their work, the way it is organised and the extent to which it is regarded as a public good or a market commodity. However, there are differences as well as similarities between the two countries. Foremost among these is the fact that New Zealand is a bicultural state. Its indigenous Māori citizens have continued to assert the importance of a Māori world view, Māori language and Māori values around education and community. The struggle for rights and recognition by Māori has influenced all aspects of policy and practice in New Zealand, including adult education.

CHAPTER THREE

Professionalism, professionalisation and continuing professional development in the adult education arena

Professionalism is not an innocent, non-political, occupational concept. It is deeply implicated in the politics of teachers' work and in the wider politics of teacher-state relations. (Lawn and Grace, 1987: x)

Introduction

The reshaping of public sector professionalism has been an aim of governments in a number of countries, including England and New Zealand. The schooling sector has been at the forefront of the struggle between practitioner and policy perspectives on professionalism since the late 1980s (Lawn and Grace, 1987; Codd, 1999, 2005; Seddon, 1997; Gewirtz and Ball, 2000; Fitzgerald, 2008; Beck, 2008, 2009). Central to this struggle are issues of control and accountability, autonomy and standards within a policy climate increasingly dominated by managerialism (S. Ball, 2000, 2003, 2008a,b, 2012). Since the late 1990s, particularly in England, the professionalising spotlight has fallen on formal post-compulsory education (Avis, 1999, 2005; Lucas and Nasta, 2010; Lucas *et al.*, 2012; Bathmaker and Avis, 2012). Although informal adult and community education has been marginal to the debate – reflecting the marginal status of adult education more generally – adult educators have not been left untouched by the discourse of professionalism, qualifications and standards.

This chapter begins by describing how different forms of 'professionalism' have been defined, refined and developed and applied to formal education more generally. It moves on to compare how policies on professionalisation and professional development have been played out in relation to adult educators in England and New Zealand. In England the focus has been on the imposition of a prescriptive form of governmental professionalism across the whole post-compulsory education sector, including adult and community-based education (Lucas and Nasta, 2010; Bathmaker and Avis, 2012). In New Zealand the focus has been on introducing a 'softer' form of professionalism, 'owned' by the sector itself, which promotes professional development as a means of enforcing greater co-ordination and standardisation of provision across the ACE sector (Tobias, 2003). In both countries, I suggest, policy pronouncements and expectations around professionalism have been utilised as a way of increasing government and (in the case of England) management control by holding out the promise of improved status and conditions for adult educators, which has not been delivered. In both countries, while the policy rhetoric about professionalisation has waned, the regulation of adult educators' work has not.

Discourses of professionalism in formal education

The literature defining professionalism and discussing its application to education is plentiful, stretching back for a century or more. This section presents four prominent discourses of educator professionalism. First it outlines a traditional or elite discourse which dominates the early literature of professionalism. It then describes the rise of a more process-oriented discourse within which continuing professional development and reflective practice are seen as important elements of the process of professionalisation. It goes on to discuss the growing prominence of a discourse of governmental or organisational professionalism from the 1990s which has shifted the policy agenda from occupational autonomy to external regulation and legislative control. This has been supported by a deficit discourse around teachers (Beck, 2008; Fitzgerald, 2008) which has characterised them as requiring professionalisation by means of greater regulation and performance management. Finally, it describes how some teacher educators, academics and teacher representatives have attempted to wrest the definition of professionalism back from policy makers and return it to practitioners, reformulated as principled or transformative professionalism. These discourses are not always easily disentangled; there are contradictions, ambiguities and overlaps between them, and it is not uncommon for one explicitly articulated discourse to mask or imply another. However, their identification helps us to 'read' policy and compare developments in different geographical, political and cultural contexts.

Traditional discourses of professionalism

Historically, the term 'professional' has been used to demarcate occupational areas on the basis of their ethos, the skills and knowledge they require for their proper performance, the autonomy they enjoy and the status they carry for the individual so named. *Traditional*, *elite* or *classical* discourses of professionalism have defined a profession by the extent to which it possesses a number of key characteristics (Flexner, 1915; Millerson, 1964; Eraut, 1994) including:

- a specialist knowledge base
- a requirement for specialised and (usually lengthy) training and study
- an ethic of public service
- a means of controlling and regulating its own membership through a recognised and autonomous professional body.

A functionalist view of professional status thus defined suggests that it provides a means by which certain groups of workers (primarily lawyers and doctors) maintain their standing in society through assurance of their competence, trustworthiness and commitment to the public good. Control of entry to – and regulation of performance within – the profession were vested in the profession itself. Professional status may also have been accompanied by a level of remuneration and respect deemed commensurate with a high social standing. A more critical view suggests that it has been a means by which a certain section of the population seeks to maintain class privilege by restricting entry to its professional ranks (Larson, 1979). There is therefore a debate to be had about whether professionalism is primarily a way of maintaining an elitist status quo. If this is the case it can be argued that the traditional formulation of professionalism cannot appropriately be applied to public service occupations, including adult education, which are associated with social justice and the equal distribution of opportunities.

51

Process discourses: *Professionalism as 'becoming'*

In the second half of the twentieth century, with the expansion of the range of jobs in the public sector requiring advanced education and training – for example in nursing, social work and teaching – definitions of professionalism became more dynamically conceived (Etzioni, 1969; Houle, 1981; Tobias, 2003). Professional status was conceptualised as a process rather than as a set of preordained criteria. Thus, while certain ethical, educational and organisational characteristics might indicate a degree of professionalism, professional status is more fluid: in the process of being achieved rather than achieved absolutely. Professionalisation (Hoyle in Gordon *et al.*, 1985) as a process of 'becoming' thus takes on a less elitist and more democratic tone, and opens up the possibility of occupational mobility for those prepared to seek it. It follows from this that those aspiring to professional status would be expected to engage in refining their skills and knowledge. It also opens the way for the promotion of professional development: '…the process whereby a practitioner acquires and improves the knowledge and skills required for effective professional practice (Hoyle, 1985: 44). Continuing professional development (CPD) and ongoing reflection on practice have therefore become part and parcel of discussion around professionalisation in the public sector generally and in education in particular (see for example Ghaye and Ghaye, 1998; Day, 1999; Roffey-Barentsen and Malthouse, 2009). However, as Tobias (2003: 148) has argued, a process definition of professionalism still remains open to the criticism that it is driven by a desire to maintain a status separation between the professional few – although rather more than in the traditional formulation – and the non-professional many. Moreover, while a process approach to professionalism may appear more democratic and fluid than a traditional approach, it opens up the possibility within the newer public sector professions of government intervention in defining what standards, training and forms of accountability might be expected of workers whose activities are prescribed by legislation and funded by government.

Government intervention and the reconstruction of professionalism

The discourse of professionalism in education has taken a new turn in the past 20 years and this has been reflected in the formal education systems of both England and New Zealand. Governmental, organisational or 'managed' professionalism (Fitzgerald, 2008; Beck, 2008, 2009; Lucas and Nasta, 2010; Bathmaker and Avis, 2012) has substituted notions of professional autonomy and self-regulation with an externally-imposed and bureaucratised version of professionalisation which can be used a tool for the exercise of managerial authority. Tanya Fitzgerald (writing from a New Zealand perspective) and John Beck (from an English perspective) have described the processes through which governmental professionalism has taken hold. First it has been predicated on casting teachers as inherently problematic, potentially incompetent and probably untrustworthy in the exercise of professional judgement. This has served to undermine their claims to autonomy and self-regulation and pave the way for regulation from above (Lucas and Nasta, 2010). Second, it has involved the government introduction of regulatory measures at all levels of educational organisation, including:

- regimes of institutional inspection and grading which differentiate institutions on the basis of their performance against externally set criteria, creating competition between them for 'customers' in an educational quasi market;
- centralised specification of curricula and qualifications and of the anticipated outcomes from education;
- bureaucratic control of teachers' qualifications, performance, conduct and ongoing training.

Governments in both countries have, by these means, been able to de-professionalise whilst claiming to professionalise, imposing external control in areas where there was formerly some professional autonomy. The dominance of governmental professionalisation has been enabled through encouraging competition between and within institutions. It has been further supported by inculcating a climate of fear among teachers, whose work is subject to constant scrutiny and individualised performance management systems, ensuring their compliance with regimes of regulation, inspection and training. It has been assisted too by the fragmentation of educators' industrial organisation (Beck, 2009) which has impeded their capacity to utilise industrial strength to resist.

'New' teacher professionalism: Responses to governmental professionalism

In response, there have been attempts to reclaim teaching as a profession. Goodson and Hargreaves, for example, try to resolve the twin issues of teachers' historical failure to gain professional recognition and the continual restructuring and direction of their work from without by distinguishing between 'professionalisation' and 'professionalism':

> *I see the project of professionalisation as concerned with promoting the material and ideal interests of an occupational group – in this case, teachers. Alongside this, professionalism is more concerned with the intricate definition and character of occupational action – in this case, the practice and profession of teaching.* (in Goodson, 2003: 126)

Goodson (2003) goes on to propose a new form of 'principled' professionalism, which he argues may emerge from the ashes of traditional professionalism (based on claims to a discrete knowledge-base) and process or 'practical' professionalism (based on the idea of the teacher as an experienced, reflective practitioner). This notion of principled professionalism, which foregrounds the ethical dimensions of teaching, is asserted as being characterised by:

- engagement with moral and social purpose
- exercise of discretionary judgement
- collaborative collegial cultures
- collaboration with parents, students and the wider community
- commitment to an ethic of care
- self-directed continuous learning
- reward for the recognition of high task complexity.

Similarly, from an Australian perspective, Judyth Sachs (2003) has attempted to salvage 'transformative' teacher professionalism, sensitive to the criticism of the elite professions and yet responsive to the policy rhetoric of 'standards', accountability and measurable outcomes. She, like Hargreaves and Goodson, asserts the possibilities for professionalism to be redefined in:

> *... more positive and principled post-modern ways that are flexible, wide ranging and inclusive in nature.* (Sachs, 2003: 35)

For Sachs this new professional identity is founded upon principles of 'learning, participation, collaboration, cooperation and activism' and stands in contrast to traditional professionalism associated with exclusivity and high status, and to governmental professionalism characterised by individualism, competitiveness and responsive to externally imposed managerialist standards. However, it may be argued (Avis, 2005) that this optimistic perspective on the possibilities for professional agency downplays the political, economic and institutional realities that constrain teachers. Further, it fails to recognise how teachers' working conditions have been reconfigured in the educational marketplace and the impact of performative regimes on their ability claim space for the kind of activist professionalism that Goodson and Sachs describe.

Policy, professionalism and adult and community education in England and New Zealand

While much has been written on the impact of policy on the professional lives of educators in the formal education system, including the post-compulsory sector (see for example Avis, 1999, 2005; Jephcote and Salisbury, 2009; Lucas and Nasta, 2010; Bathmaker and Avis, 2012; Lucas *et al.*, 2012) the challenges to educator professionalism in the non-formal adult and community education sector have received little attention in recent years. This is scarcely surprising given the contraction of adult education as a field of practice and, correspondingly, as a field of study. This section therefore focuses on the development of policy around professionalism and professional development in the field of adult and community education in England and New Zealand since the end of the 1990s. In England, community-based adult education has become caught up in the policy debates around teacher professionalism in the wider post-compulsory sector; it is therefore impossible to discuss adult and community education without reference to the sector as a whole. In New Zealand, because there has been policy recognition of adult and community education (ACE) as an area of practice distinct from the wider field of tertiary education, it is easier to untangle the specifics of ACE professional development, as will be seen below.

Policy, professionalisation and post-compulsory education in England

On the one hand the debate around professionalism in post-compulsory education in England arises from a desire on the part of educators and their trades unions to secure parity of esteem, remuneration and working conditions with school teachers (UCU, 2012). On the other hand it has arisen from a desire by government to more tightly control teacher performance. From the late 1990s concerns about the state of the UK economy and the growing policy concern around training and skills for national economic competiveness threw the spotlight on professionalism in the post-compulsory sector (Lucas and Nasta, 2010; Bathmaker and Avis, 2012; Lucas *et al.*, 2012). The reform of post-school education became a focus of the Labour administration which came to power in 1997. This was reflected in a consultation exercise on the introduction of standards and qualifications for teachers in further education (Lucas *et al.*, 2012), which led to the formation of FENTO (Further Education National Training Organisation) and the publication of national standards for teaching and supporting learning (FENTO, 1999). Following on from this, in 2001 a requirement was placed on new teachers in this sector to hold a nationally recognised and regulated teaching qualification (DfES, 2001). At the same time, inspection regimes which were already familiar in the schools sector were introduced into post-compulsory education, with the Office for Standards in Education (Ofsted) becoming responsible for learning and skills (vocational training), while the Adult Learning Inspectorate (ALI) assumed responsibility for inspecting community-based adult education provision, including local authority and voluntary sector adult education. From the outset it was therefore clear that this was governmental professionalisation from above – and that it was to be accompanied by a regime of externally imposed bureaucratic accountability.

The period from 2001 to 2007 was a hectic one in terms of moves towards governmental professionalism. In 2002 the Institute for Learning (IfL) was set up with trade union support as an independent and voluntary professional body for further education teachers, tutors and trainers. Its membership included adult and community educators as well as college lecturers in the training and skills sector. Following the publication of *Equipping our Teachers for the Future* (DfES, 2004) the IfL became fully established and from 2007 was charged by government with registering all teachers in the skills and further education sector

Table 3.1 Timeline: Governmental professionalism and post-compulsory education in England

1997–1999	• Labour government consultation on introducing standards and qualifications for further education teachers
1999	• Inauguration of FENTO (Further Education National Training Organisation) as standards body for the post-compulsory sector • Publication of sector standards for teaching and supporting learning
2001	• New teachers in the sector required to gain teaching qualification • Ofsted (Office for Standards in Education) given inspectorial role in further education • Adult Learning Inspectorate given inspectorial role in respect of adult and community education
2002	• Institute for Learning (IfL) established as the professional body for teachers in the sector, including adult and community learning • Subject specifications established for teaching in ESOL, adult literacy and numeracy following the Moser Report (DfES, 1999)
2003	• Ofsted report critical of quality of training of teachers in the sector

2004	• Government report *Equipping Our Teachers for the Future* proposed reforms to teacher training in post-compulsory sector including:
	  – requirement for new and experienced teachers – whether full-time, part-time or fractionally employed – to become qualified;
	  – requirement for teachers to undergo continuing professional development;
	  – requirement for registration with IfL for the purposes of monitoring qualifications and CPD;
	  – the promise of parity with school teaching.

2005	• Lifelong Learning UK (LLUK) replaced FENTO developing and monitoring standards across the lifelong learning sector, including ESOL, literacy, numeracy and community-based education

2006	• New standards for the sector published by LLUK • Publication of consultation on *The Professionalisation of the Learning and Skills Sector* recommending compulsory 30 hours per year CPD
2007	• Mandatory assessments published for initial teaching qualifications • The Further Education Teachers' Qualifications (England) Regulations introduced Qualified Teacher Status for the Learning and Skills Sector and a compulsory CPD requirement • Adult Learning Inspectorate merged with Ofsted
2009	• IfL five-year plan published; reports of dissatisfaction around requirement for membership of IfL • Government Report *Skills for Growth* indicated that IfL would need to become self-funding
2010	• Election of Conservative-led coalition government which confirmed requirement for IfL to become self-funding • IfL announce plan to introduce membership subscriptions to be paid by individuals
2011	• UCU boycott of IfL over imposition of compulsory subscriptions
2012	• Evaluation of teachers' qualifications in the further education sector • *Lingfield Review* of professionalism in the FE and skills sector recommended: – confirming withdrawal of funding from IfL; – revoking mandatory qualifications and CPD to be replaced by discretionary advice to employers on qualifications and CPD; – simplification of qualifications framework; – setting up of Further Education Guild – an employer-led partnership for maintaining standards and professionalism.
2013	• Government announces funding support for (employer-led) Further Education Guild

(including those working in adult and community learning) who were now required by law to qualify as teachers and to undertake a prescribed annual minimum of professional development. By this means a body set up to represent the professional interests of adult educators became co-opted into enforcing governmental professionalism. And while the kind of professionalism on offer was clearly not like that enjoyed by the traditional professions, *Equipping Our Teachers for the Future* held out to adult educators the promise of parity with school teaching, which would have been attractive to those in the post-compulsory sector subject to relatively poor terms and conditions of service:

> *The reforms set out in this document will raise the standard of teacher training across the whole sector. Over time they will result in greater public esteem for teachers, their institutions and their sector; they will help achieve joint working with schools, leading to parity of status and professionalism.* (DfES, 2004: 5)

The IfL was enthusiastic in its support of regulation as a means to professional status:

> *Now, as in other professions, CPD is seen as a hallmark of the professional and, like most professional bodies, IfL requires evidence of the individual's commitment to CPD.* (IfL, 2009: 4)

However, from 2005 onwards regulation and inspection were tightened, while educators' faith in the realisation of professional status within post-compulsory education waned. A highly critical Ofsted report (Ofsted, 2003) on standards of further education teacher training precipitated the end of FENTO and its replacement by another body, Lifelong Learning UK (LLUK), which was charged with monitoring qualifications across the whole post-compulsory sector, including ESOL, literacy, numeracy and community-based education. In another move, which was highly significant for adult education as a distinct field of practice, the ALI was abolished and Ofsted took on the inspectorial role for all educational provision, signalling an inspection regime which was likely to be less than sympathetic to the flexible and open-ended approaches favoured in community-based adult education.

As compulsion was introduced into professional registration, so the then Labour government signalled its intention to withdraw its subsidies from the IfL within three years (BIS, 2009). This meant that the IfL, if it were to survive, would need to pass costs directly on to its membership. IfL members were already becoming increasingly critical of the performance of their professional organisation (Hunt, 2011) and when the IfL introduced fees, members of the Universities and Colleges Union (which had supported the setting up of the IfL in the first place) voted to boycott the IfL. This move potentially brought adult educators in breach of the law stipulating registration with IfL as a condition of continued employment as a qualified teacher.

Matters came to a head in 2011. The recently elected Conservative-led coalition government appointed Lord Lingfield to review professionalism in the further education sector, to examine the regulations on qualifications and professional registration and to consider the functioning of the IfL (BIS, 2012a, b). The Lingfield Committee's reports were followed by further government-commissioned reports which focused on qualifications for sector workers (BIS, 2012c, d). The outcome of all this activity was the revocation of the regulations on teacher qualifications, the confirmation of the withdrawal of funding to IfL and the proposal to simplify qualifications in the sector. The Lingfield report argued for a change in the debate: 'from professionalisation of FE to supporting and enhancing professionalism which we consider already exists…' (BIS, 2012b: 6) suggesting that it 'should be a matter between employer and employee'. This was in line with the new government's strategy of deregulating some aspects of the public sector; however, it did not free educators from regimes of inspection and performance management and it has passed regulation back to employers, and not to educators themselves.

The impact on adult and community education

In all this, the work of adult and community-based educators has been rendered almost invisible by policy pronouncements, although they have been profoundly affected by the implementation of policy. The government's own reports (BIS, 2012c, d) attest to the challenges experienced in non-formal adult education, where adult educators' contracts and financial resources are frequently so constrained as to make compliance with the imposed qualifications framework unrealistic beyond a minimum required level. They also point to the shift away from non-accredited and non-vocational educational opportunities (BIS, 2012c: 45–46). The reports suggest that there is now a divide within adult and community-based education between 'compliant' organisations (which tend to be government-funded and therefore, in the main, providers of accredited and vocationally-oriented education for adults) and 'minimally-compliant' organisations, which are unlikely to be funded by government and which continue to offer non-accredited non-vocational provision. What is not clear from the limited evidence available on the qualifications of workers in English adult and community-based education is how many adult educators hold qualifications in their specialised subject area which are equivalent to, or higher than, the basic qualification required under the regulations imposed since 2001. What is clearer is that parity with school teaching has not been achieved and, more importantly for those concerned with pay and conditions rather than status, that there has been little improvement in the career prospects of adult and community educators but a significant increase in the amount of regulation laid upon them (Groves, 2012).

Professional development and adult and community education in Aotearoa New Zealand

In New Zealand the impetus to professionalise adult and community education has been more limited than in England and more focused on ACE as a distinct sub-sector. There are two possible reasons why the issue of professionalism has not had as strong an impact in Aotearoa New Zealand as it has in England. The first is that because of the historically voluntarist nature of much adult education, the number of full-time staff employed specifically in adult education work has been relatively small and scattered and as Tobias suggests:

> ... the vitality of the field of adult education was seen to rest on its voluntary character and on the fact that it was to a large extent based on the work of a diverse array of voluntary organisations as well as on the work of gifted amateurs out to change the world (Tobias, 1996a: 98)

From this perspective, forms of professionalism associated with cre-dentialisation and centralised monitoring regimes stand in opposition to transformative non-formal adult education. Second, from the late 1940s until 2011 the bulk of formally organised ACE provision was based in schools. It tended to be co-ordinated by paid staff who were school teachers, only a small portion of whose employment contracts were designated to organising educational activities for adults. They were therefore as likely to identify professionally with school teaching as with adult and community education. As in England, the majority of adult education tutors and teachers (as opposed to organisers) have been employed part time for only a few hours a week and qualified in their subject specialism rather than as teachers. The policy focus in recent years has therefore been on professional development in the ACE sector rather than professionalisation in Goodson's (2003) sense of the word.

The election of a Labour Alliance government in 1999 signalled a benign but interventionist approach to professionalism and standards in ACE. A key moment for the sector was the publication of the government-commissioned report *Koia! Koia! Towards a Learning Society: the role of Adult and Community Education* (TEC, 2001). *Koia! Koia!* acknowledged the importance of adult and community education in social, cultural, economic, community and individual development. However, it argued that the potential of ACE was underdeveloped and that the co-ordination of provision was patchy. It also suggested that the professional development of ACE practitioners – co-ordinators, organisers, tutors, managers and volunteers – had been given insufficient priority compared with other sectors of education. Capacity building, co-ordination and professional development were the key aims of a proposed strategy for the ACE sector. In order to address the professional development aims of this strategy, the Tertiary Education Commission (TEC), which was responsible for funding all forms of post-compulsory education, set up a professional development working party which co-opted practitioners working in the sector to drive forward its plans. An *ACE Professional Development Strategy and Action Plan* was published in 2005 (TEC, 2006). Its stated aim was:

> ... *to build ACE sector capacity through a well-focused and resourced approach to professional development.*

One of the key assumptions of the TEC was that the ACE sector should drive its own professional development, working in the main through regional Adult and Community Education networks. These networks, which were set up by the TEC, were seen as the key to providing local co-ordination for ACE activity and funding under the TEC's oversight.

In this sense professional development was both carrot (because it was to be funded by government) and stick (because it was predicated on expectations about regional co-ordination of the sector and the introduction of a more outcomes-based approach to ACE activity) (Bowl, 2011). Professional development was to be geared to meeting government priorities; it was to be more about sector co-ordination and rationalisation than it was about individual professionalisation.

The ACE Professional Development working party pursued the professional development strategy in the main by commissioning projects which consulted with a range of ACE organisations and individuals to identify the skills and competencies in the sector. It provided funds and support for professional development through the TEC regional networks and national conferences. It also commissioned a pilot scheme to develop a core group of regionally-based professional development 'champions' who were experienced practitioners able to offer advice and support to ACE practitioners. Some of these schemes were limited both in their impact and in their duration. Underlying problems remained: a lack of funding for ACE itself and a lack of 'buy in' from part-time, hard-pressed, poorly remunerated or unpaid adult educators to what was still essentially a top-down professional development strategy (Bowl, 2007; Synergia, 2010).

In 2008 the funding and responsibility for implementing the professional development strategy were handed over to the sector's national organisation ACE Aotearoa which continued, under TEC scrutiny, to pursue the professional development strategy. However, the rightward-leaning coalition government elected in 2009 imposed severe budget cuts to the ACE sector and revised its priorities towards supporting a much narrower range of adult education activity (TEC, 2010b). Low-level funding for regional and national professional development events continued through to 2012. ACE Aotearoa continues, too, to explore the feasibility of establishing professional standards for the sector as a whole (Prebble, 2012). ACE Aotearoa is prioritising the collection of 'quantifiable data on ACE learner outcomes' (ACE Aotearoa, 2012: 3) to persuade government of the value of adult and community education – an indication of the extent to which concerns about professional development have been overtaken by concerns about prescribing, imposing and certifying professional standards and monitoring learner outcomes. Meanwhile, the idea of a nationally-co-ordinated ACE sector with increased capacity and improved funding is far from being

Table 3.2 Timeline: Professional development and Adult and Community Education in New Zealand

2001	• Publication of *Koia! Koia!: Towards a learning society* focused on Adult and Community Education (ACE) sector capacity building and 'A managed approach to training and professional development' in the sector. Recommendations: – identification of key skills for ACE practitioners – review of training opportunities – attention to biculturalism – establishment of a Professional Development Working Group with membership from the sector and Tertiary Education Commission (TEC) to develop 'sector-led' co-ordination of professional development.
2005	• ACE Professional Development Strategy and Action Plan (2006–2010): – vision: 'success, performance and shared good practice across the sector through ACE professional development' – identification of required skills and competencies; – a 'communities of practice' approach to professional development through funding of regional ACE networks; – support for professional development 'champions' – sector-led co-ordination and strategy monitoring.
2007	• Report on ACE sector networks and professional development advocated: – a broad definition of professional development activities – consistent funding for professional development activities and professional training – paid support for part-time tutors to undertake professional development – funding for a national tutor training scheme – acknowledgment of informal professional development already taking place.

2008	• ACE Aotearoa assumes responsibility from TEC for implementation of the Professional Development Strategy responsible for: – administering grants for professional development activities among ACE organisations – sponsoring an annual *hui/fono* (conference) for Māori and Pasifika practitioners – creating web-based opportunities for professional development – distributing a Professional Development Resource Handbook for practitioners.
2009	• Election of National Party-led coalition: large-scale budget cuts in ACE provision
2010	• Evaluation of the ACE Professional Development Strategy noted: – impact of budget cuts and ACE network restructuring on plans for professional development – lack of sector infrastructure – lack of national impact of increased professional development activity.

realised as the number of schools offering ACE activities has fallen, and government subsidised adult education has declined across the board.

Summary: Professionalism: Two versions, one outcome?

In different ways adult educators in England and New Zealand have been implicated in forms of governmental professionalism. In New Zealand, particularly in the early days of the Labour Coalition, professional development policy had a softer edge. It encouraged, consulted and offered incentives. It was focused on encouraging organisations to participate in processes designed to promote greater co-ordination across a fragmented sector. It also sought to involve practitioners in defining and organising professional development to meet their own needs. While ACE organisations' participation in regional networks and their professional development activities was stipulated as a condition of receiving government funding, it was a stipulation which was not enforced: indeed it was not well enough defined to be enforced and not well enough monitored to be enforceable. More recently, however, funding cutbacks have so heavily impacted on the sector as to render the hoped-for regional co-ordination at best patchy, and at worst non-existent. In England, policy had a much harder edge and was more clearly focused on controlling individual performance by imposing tightly prescribed standards and qualification frameworks. But the current government's keenness to 'deregulate' large parts of the public sector has meant that ideology and policies of financial stringency have brought an end to direct government intervention in the professionalising project.

Table 3.3 Two government approaches to professionalism

Professionalising processes	England	New Zealand
Discourse	Professionalisation	Professional development
Mode of introduction	Imposed	Consultative
Focus	Individual performance	Sector co-ordination
Level of control	Compulsory registration/ CPD (condition of employment)	Mandatory participation (condition of funding)
Meditation	Professional association – Institute for Learning: registering body	Sector national organisation - ACE Aotearoa: co-ordination and distribution of funds

In both countries, government sought to use mediating agencies to implement policies – giving the appearance of a hands-off approach while ultimately remaining in control. In both countries, too, changes of government have precipitated policy changes which have derailed professionalising strategies. However, the centralising impetus to specify, control and measure the outcomes of adult education remains strong while the discourse of professionalisation has done little to improve the status, conditions or pay of adult educators, as Chapter Six will demonstrate.

Section Two

Adult educators' working lives researched

CHAPTER FOUR

Researching perspectives on adult education policy and practice

Life-history methods enable a focus on how teachers create educational theories within the possibilities and constraints of their circumstances – biographical, historical and political, geographical, cultural and discursive. (Middleton, 1996: 543)

Introduction

Section One described the changing context for adult education through a discussion of international developments in the field. It also described how these issues have been played out in adult education policies in England and New Zealand. Section Two focuses on the impact of this changing environment on adult educators' careers, their professional identities and their practice through an analysis of the findings of research conducted with adult educators in England and New Zealand between 2011 and 2012. In this chapter I briefly describe the rationale for taking a narrative and comparative approach to researching adult educators' work and outline how the research was conducted and how data were collected, analysed and presented.

A narrative, career history approach

A principal aim of the research was to explore adult educators' perspectives on their work and the impact of changing policy over the past 40 years through a narrative, career history approach (Middleton,

1987, 1996; Goodson, 1994; Bathmaker and Harnett, 2010). Studies of teachers' work are important in the context of changing global and national policies. First, they offer a counter-narrative to the prevailing policy discourse; in this sense they provide a means by which educators' views can be heard above the policy noise. And if, as Goodson suggests, teachers in the formal schooling system have tended to exist in the 'shadows' of policy prescriptions, this is perhaps even more the case in the non-formal sector. Adult and community-based educators tend to be casualised, marginalised and often – because of the fragmentation of the field and its lack of employee organisation – they tend not to have a political voice as an occupational group. An investigation of adult educators' perspectives places them, for once, 'at the centre of the action' (Goodson, 1994: 31). This may, on the one hand, help them to make meaning of and analyse their own experiences (Bathmaker and Harnett, 2010). On the other, it may inform those who advocate, write and make policy around adult education, offering insights into the impact of policy at community and classroom level; such insights may be more informed than those offered by commentators who sit outside the day-to-day experience of adult education. Moreover, by listening to what adult educators tell us, those committed to a broadly framed view of adult education and learning may be able to discern the possibilities for challenging dominant ideological and policy perspectives.

The questions which arise from a decision to explore the current landscape of adult education through the narratives of adult educators were therefore:

- What philosophical perspectives and professional values guide adult educators' work?
- What are adult educators' perspectives on teaching, learning and the needs and aspirations of learners who are adults?
- How do adult educators perceive their prospects as workers and their identities as professionals?
- How are adult and community educators navigating the changing policy landscape of adult education and training?
- What are the prospects for adult and community as a field of practice in the current policy climate?

A comparative approach

There are two reasons why I decided to research the perspectives of adult educators in England and Aotearoa New Zealand, countries situated at opposite ends of the globe. The first is both personal and professional. In 2006 I relocated to New Zealand, leaving a post as a manager of a community-based adult education project in England. Like many such initiatives, this project (whose staff were all employed on temporary or part-time contracts) had been sustained for the preceding ten years by a series of short-term funding sources. Having been widely recognised as successful in encouraging the educational participation of under-represented adults, the project was, for the third time in these ten years, on the verge of closure (it did indeed close later that year). The project was run under the auspices of an English university continuing education department which was itself in the throes of restructuring and subsequent closure.

In New Zealand I took up a post as a manager of an adult and community education teaching and research team based in a university continuing education department which, on the face of it, seemed to be in considerably better shape than similar contexts in England. In the wake of the election of a Labour coalition government in 1999, adult educators in New Zealand were relatively buoyant about the future, although some were cautious about the prospect of improved funding accompanying government statements of commitment to community-based, non-vocational adult education. My prophecies of doom about the way in which discourses of training, skills, credentialisation and employability were coming to dominate the field of adult education were treated with some scepticism.

In making the move to a similar setting in a different part of the world there is a temptation to compare and contrast and to explore the extent to which global trends and 'policy borrowing' (Phillips, 2009) may be mitigated or moderated by the particularities of national and cultural contexts. Whilst comparison can be problematic if it results in over-generalisation, it can also be instructive (McLean, 1992, 1995; Alexander *et al.*, 2000; Phillips and Schweisfurth, 2008; Teichler and Hanft, 2009). In the wake of a general election in 2009 the policy and funding climate for adult and community education in New Zealand deteriorated drastically (as described in Chapter Two), prompting me to consider again the extent to which adult education policy and practice are influenced by global trends and internationally dominant ideologies as well as by national historical, cultural and political contexts.

The second reason may be justified by academic and political, rather than personal, curiosity. It is widely agreed that globalisation is having an impact not just on economic relations, but on almost every aspect of national life – political, social and cultural (Giddens, 1990; Waters, 1995; UNESCO, 2001; Harvey, 2005). Globalisation entails the contraction of time and space in such a way that ideas may be rapidly transported across great distances and their influence brought to bear on local policies and practices. At the same time it is argued (Rust, in Alexander *et al.*, 2000) that globalisation does not inevitably herald homogeneity across nations. As Rust suggests in relation to education, alongside increasing global uniformity in institutional organisation, curricula and the training of teachers, attention is also paid by national governments, local communities and extra-governmental organisations to local issues of culture and diversity. Hence it seems instructive to explore the impact of globalisation on the extent to which policy 'migrates' (Phillips, 2009) to and from countries which share some aspects of a common heritage and history but which also have quite different historical and cultural antecedents. The questions which arise from a decision to explore adult education policy and practice in two countries are therefore:

- To what extent have national adult education policies and practices in England and New Zealand been influenced by global discourses?
- How have ideas, policies and practices which circulate around adult education touched down similarly or differently in England and New Zealand?
- What similarities and differences can be discerned in the values, perceptions, practices and prospects of adult educators in England and New Zealand?

The process of researching adult educators' careers

The research began in early 2011. In the main it involved the collection of narrative data from interviews with adult educators working in diverse settings in England and New Zealand. It also involved gathering information about adult education policy and practice from publicly available sources in both countries.

The adult educators

Defining adult education as a field of practice is not straightforward, and has become increasingly difficult in the context of the policy shifts and cutbacks described in Chapters One and Two. In New Zealand there is still a discernible ACE sector whose activities encompass literacy, numeracy and ESOL provision, education for personal, social and community development and Māori language and culture. Its workers are likely to be found in community, voluntary and iwi-based (Māori tribal) organisations, rural education activities programmes (REAPs), schools, colleges and universities. While the boundaries of adult education are not clear cut, it is possible to identify a cohort of workers in New Zealand who identify themselves as adult and community educators. With the exception of a small number in larger national organisations and tertiary institutions, practitioners are likely to be employed on casual, hourly-paid contracts or as unpaid volunteers. In England, cuts in funding for adult education activity which is not skills-related, together with restrictions on local government and voluntary sector expenditure, have drastically reduced the field. The concentration of funding within further education colleges catering primarily for 16- to 18-year-olds has diluted the notion of adult education, confining it largely to basic skills and ESOL or re-naming it for funding purposes as 'personal and community development learning'. Many adult educators in England have been re-designated, dispersed or displaced. However, there still remains a group of organisers, teachers and tutors, many of whom are hourly paid or self-employed, working in local authorities, colleges, universities and non-government organisations.

Participation was sought from people identifying themselves as adult educators, regardless of their employment status or context. National networks of adult educators were identified in each country and participation was sought via email through these networks. Purposive sampling (Silverman, 2000; Luttrell, 2010) was utilised to ensure that, as a whole, the participants broadly represent the field in terms of age, gender, length of experience and work context. However, the gendered nature of adult education work (particularly in face-to-face teaching) means that women make up the vast majority of those interviewed. Furthermore, I did not specifically ensure representativeness in terms of ethnicity. A snowballing approach (Hall and Hall, 1996: 109) was utilised where there were 'gaps' in offers of participation (for example, among male adult educators, educators newer to the field and educators who were not of European (Pākehā) heritage). Of 39 responses from England, and 41 from New Zealand, 31 interviews resulted in each country – a total of 62. Details of the participants in terms of their country of work, gender, length of experience and employment location are tabulated below.

Table 4.1 Research participants in England and New Zealand

		New Zealand	England
Gender	Male	3	7
	Female	28	24
Experience	0–5 years	5	3
	6–10 years	6	4
	11–20 years	10	10
	21–30 years	4	8
	31 years plus	6	6
Sector	Community/voluntary/trade union	11	4
	Local/central government	4	12
	Schools based adult and community education	4	0
	University/college	2	14
	Freelance/self-employed	10	1
Totals		31	31

A number of points are worth noting. First, the fact that women made up the overwhelming majority of those interviewed reflects the composition of the field of adult and community education – particularly those working as literacy, numeracy and ESOL teachers. To that extent the book is largely a book about women's working lives. Second, of those males who were interviewed, most were, or had been until recently, employed in full-time positions. This was in contrast to the women interviewed, the majority of whom were employed on a part-time basis (though frequently in more than one job). Again, this seems to reflect the status of women in the adult education field, and more widely in post-compulsory education, as over-represented among hourly paid, part-time or casual workers. Third, the majority of those who identified themselves as adult educators and who volunteered to be interviewed had been working in adult education for more than ten years. It was quite difficult to locate participants who were newer to the field and who regarded themselves as adult educators rather than – or as well as – lecturers, trainers or teachers within a specific setting. This may be indicative of the shift away from the notion of community-based adult educator to that of teacher or trainer based within a large institution (particularly in England) or private company (particularly in New Zealand). It also reflects the general decline in adult education as a recognised field of practice.

Fourth, differences in employment settings between New Zealand and England are apparent, reflecting historical differences in the structuring of adult and community education, as well as the more recent policy developments in the two countries. The majority of those adult educators interviewed in New Zealand were employed in the voluntary or community sectors or in schools or were working on a freelance basis. Schools-based adult education (which had been one of the strongest areas for ACE practice) was in decline as a result of the recent government cuts in funding (discussed in Chapter Two). A number of those interviewed had recently moved from the schools sector to self-employment. Moreover, in New Zealand the majority of ESOL and literacy provision was organised by two major non-government organisations (Literacy Aotearoa and English Language Partners). In England ESOL and basic skills provision is now mainly based in further education colleges; schools-based adult education has been a rarity in recent years. At the time of the interviews some local education authorities were still offering adult education provision, but were in the throes of reorganisation and retrenchment as a result of local government funding cuts. While any claims for the 'generalisability' of the findings from interviews with these adult educators are made with considerable caution, every attempt was made to ensure a spread of participation across the sectors in both countries and the interviews are illustrative of what appeared to be the situation at the time they took place.

The interviews

Wherever possible tape-recorded face-to-face interviews were conducted. However, for reasons of availability and geography (particularly in

New Zealand where distances are often long and travelling by public transport can be a challenge) it was sometimes necessary to conduct telephone, Skype or email interviews. The interview questions were broadly similar in all cases and participants were invited to discuss:

- their career trajectories as adult education practitioners – how they came into the field of adult education, what training they had undergone, what work they had undertaken in the past and how they were currently employed;
- their philosophies and values as adult educators – how they viewed themselves as teachers, their relationships with adult learners and what they saw as the aim and purpose of their efforts;
- the ways in which their practice had changed over the course of their careers – the extent to which changing policy and funding had an impact on their philosophy and values, their relationships with adult learners, their colleagues, their employers and their approach to their work;
- the perceived challenges and opportunities for adult education in the next ten years – how they saw themselves as adult educators in the future and how they saw their career prospects.

The interviews took place over the period between May 2011 and January 2012, during which time different policy changes were having an impact on the adult and community education sectors in the two countries. In England, changes to the funding of ESOL provision and a dispute around the enforced 'professionalisation' of the post-compulsory sector (discussed in Chapter Three) were ongoing. In New Zealand, widespread cuts and changed priorities and targets in the adult and community education sector were still being worked through on the ground. The preoccupations of the adult educators in the two countries reflected the specifics of the local policy contexts.

Analysing the interview data

Data were analysed for recurrent or contrasting themes across contexts, lengths of experience, and other factors differentiating between adult educators, and for cross-country differences and similarities (Wolcott, 1994). The themes which guided the writing of Chapters Five to Eight were:

- adult educators' philosophies: how beliefs and values guided their practice and the extent to which they felt their practice was informed by adult education theory;
- the idea of a career in adult education: how adult educators entered and trained for their careers, how they viewed their work and their career prospects;
- adult educator agency and resistance: how experienced adult educators accommodate or resist policy directives that conflict with their beliefs about the purpose of adult education;
- strategic responses to changes in the structure and funding of adult education: how adult educators and the organisations advocating for adult education respond to changing policy and increasing financial stringency.

In Chapter Five I use extracts from a number of the interviews to demonstrate the range of philosophical positions among, and the differences in emphasis between, adult educators in England and New Zealand. In Chapter Six I focus on portraits of early-, mid- and late-career adult educators in both countries to illustrate the impact of career uncertainty at different stages in their working lines. Similarly, in Chapter Seven I have focused on the narratives of particular individuals, this time four experienced adult educators, as their stories suggest how adult educators work with or against policy which they see as hampering their work. In Chapter Eight I use short extracts from a number of interviews to illustrate the strategic considerations of adult educators in the two countries.

In presenting the analysed data I have considered the ethics of portraying the feelings and perspectives of others and taken as my 'acid test' Sikes' (2010) question – how I would feel if my own narrative were portrayed? I have therefore removed hesitations and digressions where they have seemed to be irrelevant to what the interviewee was trying to say. I have also removed identifying information as far as possible, without changing the individual's narrative.

Documentary sources

Adult educators' identities are shaped by social and political contexts as well as personal biography. Another aim of the research was to explore adult educators' experiences within these contexts (Jephcote and Salisbury, 2009). During the period when the interviews were being conducted, policy in both countries continued to change. Publicly available documentary sources on the development of adult education policy and practice in England and New Zealand have therefore been accessed. These include published and unpublished reports, policy documents, conference proceedings, campaign briefings and newsletters.

Summary

This chapter has described my personal, professional, political and academic reasons for undertaking research with adult educators in two countries which have close ties but different geographical, cultural and historical contexts. In addition, it has explained why a narrative, career history approach was taken to examining the working lives of adult educators. The chapters which follow are based primarily on data gathered from semi-structured interviews with 62 adult educators – evenly split between the two countries – working full-time, part-time or in a voluntary capacity and in a variety of settings. They also draw on published and unpublished documentary material which provides information about the context for adult educators' practice. The remaining chapters in this book are informed by themes emerging from the research and seek to offer an account which foregrounds the perspectives of adult educators on the current state of adult education in England and New Zealand.

CHAPTER FIVE

Adult educator philosophies and values

Adult education is an exceptionally diverse field whose practitioners do not all share a common professional culture, or even a common term to designate what it is they do. Debates among adult educators are accordingly informed – or ill-informed – by an inadequate theoretical base and distorted by terminological and conceptual confusions. Where these debates are concerned with vital political questions of direction, purpose, the exercise of power and the allocation of resources, theoretical weakness can have serious practical consequences, making it hard for practitioners to understand the situations in which they find themselves and unsure what action to take. Where politics is concerned, while knowledge may not always be power, ignorance is rarely bliss. (Coben, 1998: 5)

I'm low on educational theories but my favourite quote is 'If you think education is expensive, try ignorance'. (Rita, England, part-time literacy and ESOL teacher, eight years)

Introduction

The introductory chapter referred to the literature which discusses the values, beliefs and theories underpinning adult educators' work and the frameworks for analysis proposed by Apps (1973), Heimstra (1988), Zinn (1990), Elias and Merriam (1994) and others who suggest that adult educators are likely to draw on differing philosophical traditions to direct their practice. A distinction is made in some of the adult education literature between individualistic and collectivist conceptions of adult education (Armstrong and Miller, 2006). This chapter develops that discussion and presents data from the research carried out with adult educators in New Zealand and England in which they talk about their value orientations, their relationship to theory and the extent to which they saw theory as influencing their practice.

At the outset, however, it seems reasonable to define what a philosophical perspective entails in relation to adult education, and whether an explicit understanding of the values and principles that guide adult educators is important to practice. It may be argued that adult education is, above all, a practical pursuit; practitioners (often working in insecure and hourly-paid employment) may have little time or inclination to link their practice to abstract theorising. Yet whether or not it is articulated, a philosophical orientation underlies the practices and policies of both individuals and institutions. Merriam and Brockett define a philosophical perspective in relation to education as:

> *A conceptual framework, embodying certain values and principles that renders the educational process meaningful... A philosophy of education typically includes discussion of terms, aims and objectives, curricula, methods, the teaching–learning transactions, the role of society, and the role of student and teacher.* (1997: 28)

Working from a philosophical perspective involves recognising that there is a link between theory (abstract frameworks for informing understanding), values (systems of belief) and practice (daily activity in adult education), and acknowledging that:

- adult education is a purposeful practice, underpinned (tacitly or explicitly) by beliefs;
- beliefs about the purposes of adult education should be communicated between educators and learners in order to establish common understandings of the aims of any particular adult education activity; doing so will be beneficial in promoting learning;
- adult educators have choices about how they approach their practice, how they relate to learners and how they plan and carry out their teaching; values and beliefs help to provide a framework for making these choices;

- choices may be constrained or dictated to a greater or lesser extent by the values, beliefs and regulations set by others within the context for practice;
- having an understanding of their own aims and purposes enables adult educators to recognise the tensions and contradictions between their beliefs and the expectations laid upon them and to make an appropriate judgement about how to act in these circumstances.

However, an individual's philosophical beliefs are not independent of the social and political context, nor are they fixed and immutable. They are constructed and reconstructed in changing social and political conjunctures, through interaction with others and through external influence and personal reflection. They may not be consciously articulated – they may even be denied. But, consciously or otherwise, they provide a context for practice.

Philosophy and values in the literature of adult education

There is a wealth of literature which suggests that adult educators align to discrete philosophical positions, each with its own theoretical stance and view of the learner, learning and the educator. These positions have arisen from particular historical, political and social circumstances. From the frameworks proposed by Apps (1973), Heimstra (1988), Zinn (1990) and Elias and Merriam (1994) five main philosophical traditions are identified: liberalism, behaviourism, progressivism, humanism and radicalism. Each view is briefly summarised below:

- *Liberalism* is associated with the idea of developing a cultured and knowledgeable individual for whom learning 'for its own sake' is the goal. It has underpinned liberal adult and continuing education and particularly university continuing education.
- *Behaviourism*, founded on experimental psychology, characterises learning as an observable response to behavioural conditioning, managed through expert instruction, whose outcomes are observable. The approach has long been used in contexts where control or remediation of behaviour has been a goal (for example, in

penal and rehabilitative settings). It has gained ascendency in recent years in the adult training sector through the development of outcomes-based assessment frameworks (Hyland, 1994).

- *Progressivism/pragmatism*, founded on Dewey's (1938) ideas, promotes learner-centred teaching, and learning through a practical, problem-solving approach, which has as its aim the development of knowledge and skills that contribute to social development and democracy. As J. Irwin (2012: 7) has pointed out, in recent years pragmatism has also been distorted to advance instrumentalism in education.
- *Humanism*, drawing on Carl Rogers (1969), has as its focus personal growth and development, arrived at through the non-directive intervention of the educator as skilled facilitator who, in turn, will contribute to a more humane society. This approach has been prominent in therapeutic educational contexts and in programmes aimed at supporting personal development.
- *Radicalism* in adult education has its roots in anti-colonial and anti-imperialist struggles (Freire, 1972; Nyerere, 1976) as well as in organised labour, socialist and co-operative movements (Gramsci, 1971; Lovett, 1988). Radical approaches are directed towards the collective development of knowledge and understanding as a means of bringing about social change and restructuring power relations. In the United Kingdom and New Zealand radical adult education has been associated with political activism around feminist, anti-colonial, anti-apartheid, anti-racist and anti-war struggles and, in New Zealand, around the struggle for Māori self-determination. Adult education research and literature retains a radical discourse with writers such as Thompson (1997), Foley (1999, 2001), Martin (2005) and others contributing to a critique of policy developments over the past 25 years.

Another way of conceptualising adult educators' philosophies has been to distinguish between individual and social purposes (Armstrong and Miller, 2006). An individual orientation encompasses consideration of learners' rights, responsibilities, wants and needs and how education can be used to ensure that these are met. It might include consideration of the specific needs of individual learners who fall into particular groups – by virtue of their age, ethnicity, gender or previous educational experience. A social orientation encompasses consideration of how

82

education functions to maintain or transform social relations. Within a social orientation, Armstrong and Miller make a further distinction between a liberal notion of social purpose – as support for social order and 'social control' – and a more radical, collective perspective which seeks 'to challenge the hegemony and dominant ideologies of the ruling classes, as well as of patriarchy' (Armstrong and Miller, 2006: 293). Again, shifts in policy to a more economically-focused view of adult education and lifelong learning make problematic these conceptions of adult educator philosophy as does the tendency (which Armstrong and Miller also note) for the terminology of radical, socially-focused aims to be transformed for different ends by conservative and neoliberal policy discourses. Thus, for example, the concept of empowerment has taken on a very different meaning from that which it held in Freirean-influenced radical educators' discourse and is commonly used to signify individual well-being, rather than the collective struggle for political and social change. Likewise, the notion of lifelong learning has (as discussed in Chapter One) shifted from a social right to an economic necessity.

Attempts to categorise distinct philosophical orientations are not unproblematic. They imply a consistency which may not accord with the day-to-day realities of practice; adult educators may work in a range of settings or for a range of purposes at any one time, or over the course of their careers. Moreover, the social and political milieux in which philosophical positions emerge shift over time, as do the interpretations placed on these positions. For example, a progressive/pragmatist approach may, as suggested above, be reinterpreted in policy terms as less radical and more instrumental than originally intended in Dewey's conceptualisation; and claims to be engaged in education for empowerment may not necessarily be radical in their intention.

Rather than seeing these perspectives as distinct and clear-cut, it may perhaps be more realistic to consider adult educators' philosophical out-looks in terms of a spectrum of belief – from more or less oriented to the status quo (conservative) to more or less oriented to social change (radical) (see Figure 5.1), acknowledging that these positions themselves are open to change as already mentioned. In this configuration a conservative view would conceptualise the learner as needing to work within the prevailing socio-economic system, taking responsibility for their own educational success or failure and the teacher as offering (for a price) the means to attain success, as measured in qualifications. A liberal/humanist perspective would conceptualise the learner with abilities which may be developed (with the help of the educator) for the purpose of individual or social advancement and improvement. A radical perspective, on the other hand, would reject the idea that the purpose of education is individual or social improvement or advancement. Rather, the radical educator is an activist for social change, working alongside other activist learners-as-teachers for change (Freire, 1972).

Figure 5.1 A spectrum of beliefs and values?

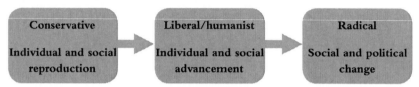

While different approaches may co-exist, within a particular policy constellation one may become dominant. From the discussion in Chapters One and Two of the policy shifts which have taken place in the field of adult education and lifelong learning over the past 30 years, it is relatively easy to discern that the prevailing policy climate for adult education has been characterised by a shift away from liberal and humanist notions of adult education's aims and purposes and towards more conservative instrumentalist and outcomes-focused approaches. And while a radical perspective on adult education's purpose may have been maintained in contexts in which the focus was on nation-building and throwing off the legacy of imperialism, these ideas have never held sway in the policy discourse of industrialised countries such as England and New Zealand. The possibility of there being some disjunction between adult educators' philosophies of practice and policy aims for lifelong learning is therefore strong.

Practitioner beliefs and values

In this section I explore how adult educators described the beliefs and values guiding their practice. What has emerged is a more complex picture than that suggested in the literature, in which biography, ideology and experience combined to shape the adult educators' perspective on the purpose of their work. As demonstrated below, these adult educators took a variety of positions focused on individual development and advancement – which could be described as primarily liberal/

humanistic. They included those who took a view of adult education as compensating for past negative educational experiences and those whose perspectives were informed by a community development approach. There was also a group of practitioners of longstanding whose perspectives were informed by radical ideas – although it will be noted that some of these practitioners' positions had been re-shaped in the prevailing policy environment.

Individually-focused perspectives

Absent from adult educators' descriptions of their philosophical positions was a conservative, behaviourist or instrumentalist standpoint. Most prominent was a broadly liberal/humanist perspective (Merriam and Brocket, 1997), with practitioners stressing their role in supporting individual development. Adult education was characterised as a process of self-actualisation (Rogers, 1969) and the adult educator's role was characterised as facilitating learners to articulate and pursue their own learning aims:

> *I think I take a fairly humanistic approach, in that I feel I work towards a learner-centred approach which is in line with the current thinking in adult education… I think that everyone should have the chance to get the education that they want whoever they are and at whatever level and that people should be allowed to learn for the sake of learning not just because their job requires it or that it will lead to work.* (Moira, England, full-time adult educator, five years)

> *You put your learner at the heart of whatever you do. The learner comes first; don't impose anything upon them. What do they want? How do they want it delivered? What are their barriers? Look at finding ways that enable them to do it. Everyone should have the opportunity to learn or to have that second opportunity.* (Denise, England, full-time adult education co-ordinator, 25 years)

> *I think it's that people need something and I've got some skills that will meet those needs. It has to be needs based.* (Edith, New Zealand, part-time ESOL tutor, ten years)

The notion of learner-centred teaching was strongly articulated. Focusing on the learners' needs, interests, abilities and aims was seen as central, particularly among adult educators working in the field of literacy and language teaching. This perhaps reflects the more individualised approach in these areas, particularly where it is still possible (as, for example, in some ESOL teaching in New Zealand, and in literacy support more generally) to work on a one-to-one basis with learners without the pressure of accreditation. In larger group classroom settings a learner-centred approach would entail eliciting, acknowledging and responding to the different needs of learners and encouraging their active engagement in identifying and realising their own learning aims. The extent to which this is feasible within a policy climate which is increasingly prescriptive in terms of curriculum and assessment may be open to question.

Among those expressing a primarily liberal/humanist perspective, the concept of 'empowerment' featured strongly with reference to individual, rather than collective learning. This suggests the influence of theoretical approaches, such as that of Rogers (1969), which advocate person-centeredness and self-direction. The attractions of this approach for adult educators working with learners characterised as vulnerable, disadvantaged or lacking in confidence are clear. Its therapeutic tone lends a sense of mission to work with adult learners who have had difficult life and educational experiences. However, empowerment thus characterised stands in danger of losing its dialogic sense (Freire, 1972) and being stripped of some of its socio-political meaning (Brookfield, 2005).

Compensatory perspectives: Redressing exclusion and disadvantage

Those who took a primarily individualistic view of adult education's purpose were also often informed by a commitment to adult education as a vehicle for compensating for social disadvantage. Here, social and individual purposes overlapped and intertwined; individually-focused perspectives were infused with commitments to equal opportunities and second chances:

> *The theoretical bit is all the stuff around experiential learning and linking in living and doing; and it's also the second chance learning that connects to my own roots. I am certainly from a background that is not much different from the students; I just handled it differently. It's about that and helping people to be – not the best that they can*

86

be – but making the most of each day. (Gloria, New Zealand, full-time adult education manager, 30 years plus)

Compensatory perspectives were particularly apparent among the English adult educators. This perspective was frequently referenced to past personal or family disadvantage:

> *Adult education for me is for people who have had the compulsory education experience; hated it, because I did; then they've come out the other side: what are we going to do now? Where am I going?* (Fiona, England, full-time literacy co-ordinator, 15 years)

> *I'm the only person in my family with an 'O' Level even and I seem to be able to communicate very well with people... I've got this sort of communication skills because my own family struggled with reading and writing. I liked the way it built people's confidence; it opened doors... I guess it's that sort of: helping people to make things happen.* (Cathy, England, part-time tutor/teacher trainer, 25 years)

A striking aspect of the interviews was the extent to which adult educators drew on their own negative memories of schooling and how these experiences shaped their view of the importance of 'second chances'. Embedded in these perspectives was a tacit criticism of the failure of compulsory schooling to engage and reward all its pupils. It raises questions as to why adults should be seen to have been failed by the compulsory education system on such a scale as to warrant compensation for their lost opportunities. It also suggests that, beneath the discourse of 'lifelong learning for all' is a story of the failure of formal compulsory education to offer equal chances.

Community-focused perspectives

Among New Zealand adult educators the themes of community development and social cohesion were particularly strong. In England they were almost completely absent. This may reflect a number of factors specific to New Zealand. First, the more rural and closely net-worked nature of New Zealand may have encouraged a focus on community cohesion. This has been reflected in government funding of REAPs, whose focus has combined adult education and community development approaches. Second, it may reflect, in the minds of adult educators, the 1999–2008 Labour-led government's commitment to adult education's role in promoting community development and social cohesion (TEC, 2007) and in particular its concern for the successful social integration of growing numbers of new migrants and refugees. Third, it may reflect the importance of the influence of community- and family-focused approaches of Māori and Pasifika practitioners.

> *My main value or philosophy is about bringing people together.*
> *I feel most learning happens when people have the opportunity*
> *to come together – social cohesion, shared learning…There are so*
> *many reasons for doing these local community-based courses and*
> *collaborative, cohesive communities have to be the most important.*
> (Hilary, New Zealand, part-time co-ordinator, 17 years)

> *I think that if you look at ACE without the community development*
> *you would miss the crucial part of needs analysis and empowering*
> *people to take control and identify their own issues. And if you*
> *get that right, ACE can flourish. But if you prescribe what people*
> *need you are not going to get real sustainable results… The 'Es' of*
> *community – educating, empowering and enlivening. Over my career*
> *I guess it was also about equity; that people often know where they*
> *want to go, they just require the tools to get there. And underlying*
> *and underpinning that is education in the broadest sense.* (Deirdre,
> New Zealand, full-time REAP co-ordinator, 30 years plus)

> *It's definitely about community development and enabling people*
> *to function better in the community… To work with the whole*
> *person and their family… We are there to help them make the often*
> *extremely difficult transition to living in the new country.* (Debbie,
> New Zealand, part-time ESOL tutor, 12 years)

> *My family are Māori, my kids are Māori, and so I have lived in that*
> *kind of community… And it's the holistic approach. It's not just that*
> *the whole community needs to raise a child; the whole community*
> *needs to bring in the young adult – and the older adult.* (Caroline,
> New Zealand, full-time ACE organiser, two years in practice)

In New Zealand, changing government policy on adult and community education presents challenges for adult and community educators whose perspectives are expressed in terms of community development. The shift towards targeting specific learner groups, to compensatory education, language and literacy teaching and to promoting progression to more formal tertiary education (Ministry of Education, 2010) represents a change in tone around social and community development and cohesion which is likely to challenge adult educators' values and have an impact on their practice.

Radical perspectives

Radical perspectives were only apparent from the interviews with some of those adult educators, in both countries, who had been in the field for 25 years or more. This was scarcely surprising given that, as described in Chapters One and Two, the period between the late 1960s and early 1980s was when radical ideas were influential internationally and this radicalism was reflected in adult education and community work training. This minority of most experienced practitioners cited theoretical influences such as Freire, Illich and Nyerere motivating them to become adult educators and guiding their practice. Interestingly, none mentioned Gramsci. They articulated a more overtly political view of the role of adult education as a force for social and economic change:

> … *for me it was really both a non-violent means for bringing about social change and it was also a way of allowing voices to be heard that had not been heard.* (Ann, New Zealand, full-time unpaid educator, 30 years plus)

> *I guess it's that whole Freirean thing. This critical pedagogy; that's where I'm at I'd say. I'm very committed to that.* (Sue, England, full-time ESOL Teacher, 25 years)

These adult educators traced the roots of their radicalism through their biographies – histories of trade union, anti-colonial and community activism and associations with political and social movements. Their philosophical positions, grounded in their experience, were clearly at odds with the thrust of current policy. This was recognised by some, who had had to manage the tension between long-held beliefs and dominant values. Brian had reassessed his philosophical position and recognised the ideological shift he had made:

> *I have at the age of 58 had to learn to live with the fact that I've been living a lie all my life: this notion that I would always see myself as an educator in the Freirean model, an educator for social change. But I can't exactly look around and see what successes I've had… It's a source of confusion in my own head to a certain extent, because we were children of the view that we would change the world – and the things we thought we would change, we have not changed. And some of those forces we thought were for the good were not for the good.* (Brian, England, full-time adult educator, 30 years plus)

For adult educators expressing a radical perspective on their work the contradictions between values and ideals and the expectations of practice were the sharpest. Some, like Brian, shifted their perspective in ways which aligned with prevailing policy, emphasising, instead of radical social change, equality of opportunity and compensation for past educational and social harm.

> *The irony is that shifting to a training model I think 'upped the ante' in terms of the quality of teaching and learning. There would be all sorts of caveats to that which I would make, but I would say that today [the centre] meets its mission to promote social justice far more effectively than it did when it was running around screaming about: 'this is what we do'. Because people that now come here… You're talking about people who are not just working class; they are people who have been trashed by the system, as well as being working class. To connect with that kind of multiple disadvantage… has upped my personal skills, upped my conceptual models in all sorts of ways.* (Brian)

Brian's narrative demonstrates how educators' value systems may be re-articulated in order to cope with the contradictions which arise from changing ideological climates (Jephcote and Salisbury 2009). Others, like Anne and Sue, maintained their radical stance. Benn and Burton (1995) in their analysis of interviews with adult educators in the UK who were teaching adult students on Access to Higher Education courses suggested that, while adult educators may espouse radical and emancipatory approaches, their rhetoric tends to be contradicted by their descriptions of practice. Commitment to collective action and egalitarianism may be forced into the background by other imperatives – in particular government policy and funding regimes.

Adult educators' relationships to theory

It is often suggested that adult educators tend to shy away from theory in favour of focusing on the practical demands of the work (Coben, 1998; Ledwith, 2007; Bowl, 2010) – a tendency which has been identified as problematic. At best it may tend to blunt debate and critical analysis of practice. At worst, it may foster an anti-intellectualism, which runs counter to the idea of education as the development of critical awareness. Margaret Ledwith argues that by failing to engage critically with the causes and effects of social injustice in the wider world, practitioners may, by omission, be contributing to perpetuating it:

> We need to be vigilant and stay critical if we are to prevent
> our practice getting distracted and slipping into some feel-good,
> ameliorative sticking plaster on the wounds of injustice. (Ledwith,
> 2007: 4)

Furthermore, as Coben (1998: 5) has suggested, 'theoretical weakness' may leave practitioners vulnerable to ideologically driven attacks on their work; they may lack the tools to articulate their purpose, beyond a generalised commitment to an ethic of care and personal development. This section therefore examines the extent to which adult educators in this research embraced or eschewed theory. In addition, it discusses the main theoretical influences mentioned and some of the different ways they were interpreted. In particular, interpretations of Paulo Freire – the theoretical influence who was most widely cited – will be discussed.

Attitudes to theory

Theoretical influences did not feature strongly in liberal/humanist adult educators' accounts of their values and beliefs. The one exception to this was the extent to which, as discussed above, Carl Rogers (1969) was cited in relation to person-centred approaches. However, a range of influences were mentioned in answer to a specific interview question about theorists. These covered theories of learning and teaching as well as socio-political theories of education and the role of the educator. Social constructivist approaches to teaching and learning among children (as exemplified by Bruner, 1960 and Vygotsky, 1978) were cited as informing practice which took into account the social situation in the classroom and adults' prior knowledge and experience. Despite the popularity of Malcolm Knowles's (1973) work on 'andragogy' during the 1970s, there was little mention of it. There was also no mention of those writers, for example Gramsci or Giroux, whose work commonly features in academic discussion of the public role of the adult educator. However, a range of specialised teaching approaches and techniques was cited, including the Suzuki and Feldenkras methods, Stephen Krashen's (1982) work on second language acquisition and Frank Smith's work on *Writing and the Writer* (1994).

There was reluctance on the part of some to consider theoretical influences at all. This was either because theory was seen as distant and over-elaborated, or else because it was felt that, since 'everyone is different', theory was too prescriptive:

> *It's more a pragmatic approach and our students are so different, and they come from such different places that you can't just say: this is the approach. This is my problem with a lot of the trendy things because a) I don't have access to the time or materials and b) they might suit some students I have, but I don't think they would suit [them all].*
> (Ellen, England, part-time ESOL teacher, 30 years plus)

> *Despite having finished my MA I find a lot of theoretical writing about education uninspiring and sometimes written in such complex language it is clearly only meant for academics. The learners, practitioners through forums, networks and our own teams I think are the most important sources of inspiration for me.* (Olivia, England, full-time adult educator, 28 years)

In general, adult educators who were newer to the field were less likely to discuss theoretical influences than those who were practitioners of long standing or who had studied adult education or community work in a university setting. But this was not always the case. Some of those who had earlier in their careers been influenced by adult education theorists had reverted to more pragmatic approaches:

I haven't drawn on any one theory in particular. I guess my philosophy is that education should be learner-based and participant-driven. (Deirdre, New Zealand, full-time REAP co-ordinator, 30 years plus)

I went through Malcolm Knowles and andragogy, and realised how it was trying to make something different and distinct and it didn't really work. But I liked his style, and I liked what he was trying to do. But since then, I've been a bit chary of any kind of theorists, to be frank. And I've spent all my time working on what works. And it's actually being very practical about things. (Alan, England, retired adult educator, 30 years plus)

Most interesting was the apparent lack of impact of recent writing and theorising around adult and popular education. This may reflect the way in which adult educator training itself is changing to a more competence-based and less theoretically driven curriculum. It may also highlight a wider disengagement from academic debate reflected in neoliberalism's anti-intellectual thrust (Giroux, 2001, 2006). It should give pause for thought to academics communicating and disseminating their work to practitioners and the wider public.

Interpretations of Freire
Paulo Freire was the one theorist who was widely cited by adult educators in both countries. Interpretations of his legacy in practice varied widely from notions of individual empowerment to a more socio-political perspective. For example, one adult educator explained Freire's influence on her in relation to learner-centredness and self-direction:

I'm definitely very interested in Paulo Freire, and his learner-centred approach and more than that in terms of what he speaks about regarding the learner's cultural capital and how that empowers people to find learning for themselves. (Beth, New Zealand, full-time adult educator, 15 years)

Practitioners working in literacy and language learning also mentioned aspects of Freire's work as it applied to their approach to class teaching. Judith, for example, had been informed by Freire's concept of 'generative themes' (Freire, 1972: Ch. 3). This refers to the educator eliciting topics and concerns which are of immediate political or cultural significance to learners and utilising these as the basis for class discussion and learning. Judith's interpretation of this is focused on building on learners' experiences and interests (which echoes social constructivism as much as radical theory):

> *He uses this phrase: generative words. That is a very interesting concept which I drew on extremely heavily to start with. And I think it's very important in adult education… That's the ideal. Obviously I'm working in a second language. I try and identify what comes up and what they might be interested in, and what's useful for them. And also the other thing which is the Language Experience approach, which is very useful. And that is related, isn't it? Ideally, you might, in a similar way, take topics which are very interesting for the students; very dear to their hearts. Take their words, or something like their words.* (Judith, England, full-time ESOL teacher, 25 years)

Beth and Judith suggest the different ways in which Freire can be interpreted and applied to practice. Just as Ledwith (2007) has cautioned that radical ideas and concepts may be turned to non-radical ends, Bob, in his interview, expresses a similar sentiment when looking back on his career as an adult educator influenced by Freirean ideas:

> *It was that notion that Freirean education could not be stripped of its social and ideological context; and that if you pretended that education didn't have a sociological and ideological context, you were in fact engaged in oppressive education… And Freire would be turning in his grave now.* (Bob, England, full-time adult education manager, 30 years plus)

The evidence suggests a limited engagement on the part of adult educators with the political dimension of Freire's work and an emphasis on teaching techniques rather than critical pedagogy – a tendency which Freire himself warned against (Freire, 1985; Allman, 1988).

Summary: Philosophies, values and theories

There has been a tendency in the literature to suggest that adult educators' beliefs and values can be assigned to discrete philosophical positions. The perspectives of adult educators presented above suggest a more fluid picture, with individual- and socially-oriented motivations often intertwined and sometimes shifting. Conservative, instrumentalist or behaviourist influences were absent. Predominantly, adult educators' values and beliefs were expressed in liberal/humanist terms with a concern to direct their efforts towards promoting equality of opportunity and compensating for past educational disadvantages. In the case of New Zealand-based practitioners, a community- and socially-oriented perspective was more strongly evident than in England where a compensatory discourse seems to have a strong hold.

Expressions of a radical perspective were confined to those adult educators who had been longest in practice and influenced by the adult education ideas of the 1960s and 1970s. However, among some, these perspectives had shifted towards an orientation more closely aligned to policies targeting specific disadvantaged groups and individuals. While there were differences between the radical educators and the rest in the extent to which they drew on theory to explain their philosophical approach, ethics of fairness and equality threaded through almost all accounts. And for most there was a disjunction between their expressions of their philosophy and policy discourses of markets, targets and inspection which they went on to describe in their day-to-day work.

Overall, these adult educators described their practice as being informed by personal and professional experience, rather than as explicitly underpinned by theory. There was some reluctance to engage in theoretical analysis of the ideological context within which adult education is being re-shaped. This reluctance leaves adult educators vulnerable to shifts in ideology and policy, in the way that Coben (1998) suggests. These finding underline the importance of revitalising dialogue between those who critique policy and those who are expected to enact it (Giroux, 2001, 2006). While it might be hypothesised that individual practitioners working on a daily basis are bound to take a pragmatic approach to their work, it does raise the question of how the adult educators manage conflicting perspectives and what happens when policy shifts marginalise humanist or socially-oriented perspectives and promote more individual instrumentalist ends, as in the current climate. To what extent are they able to exercise agency (Emirbayer and Mische, 1998; Lawy and Tedder, 2009) in situations where the dominant policy thrust is at odds with their beliefs? Chapter Seven will explore this question in the light of the discussion of adult educators' expressed philosophical positions.

CHAPTER SIX

A 'non-career': Occupational identities and career trajectories

I feel like a polar bear sitting on an iceberg which is slowly melting. My environment is being slowly whittled away, and what's left of it is not enough to make a living. I'm virtually unemployed in a sense.
(Carla, England, part-time adult educator and volunteer, 30 years plus)

I think the first point I'd make is that it's definitely a non-career.
(Imogen, New Zealand, part-time adult educator and volunteer, 30 years plus)

Introduction

Fifty years ago, it was possible to define a 'career' as: 'A succession of related jobs, arranged in a hierarchy of prestige, through which persons move in an ordered, predictable sequence' (Wilensky, 1960: 127, cited in Sikes *et al.*, 1985). While such a predictable progression has rarely characterised women's working lives it now seems more generally unthinkable from the perspective of a globalised and marketised economic and political climate. Historically, too, a career in the public sector was associated with a balance between a service ethic and a degree of job security and public respect. But since the 1980s, government pressures to drive down public sector expenditure and to restructure public service provision have resulted in work intensification, loss of job security and increasing demoralisation among public sector workers (De Ruyter *et al.*, 2008).

97

At the same time the 'flexible', 'portfolio' or 'contingent' worker has become an established feature of the employment scene in much of Europe, North America, Australia and New Zealand (Handy, 1994; Feldman, 2006). The deterioration in adult educators' job security needs to be seen against the background of attacks on workers' rights and trade union organisations from the early 1980s onwards (Kirk and Wall, 2011). Both are manifestations of the same ideological thrust.

In this context, the careers of educators in the formal schooling and tertiary sectors have received a good deal of research attention over the years (Ball and Goodson, 1985; Sikes *et al.*, 1985; Day, 1999; Avis, 1999; Kirk and Wall, 2011). This is not the case in adult education. The casualised nature of adult educators' work reflects not only its voluntarist roots but also the historical marginality of concerns about education beyond compulsory school age. Moreover, there has been a tradition whereby evening classes for working people have been taught by educators who had day jobs elsewhere. Therefore, arguably, remuneration levels were not a priority (Tobias, 1996a; Osborne and Sankey, 2009). However, adult education has been the sole or main occupation of some in both England and New Zealand and it is strange when one considers the policy preoccupation with the professionalisation and professional development of adult educators (discussed in Chapter Four) that so little attention has been paid to their working lives and conditions. Against the wider background of increasing job insecurity, this chapter explores what it means to have a career in adult education through the narratives of six adult educators in England and New Zealand who are at different stages in their working lives. Their stories exemplify some of the challenges to the notion of a career in adult education – the haphazard nature of entry into the field, the opportunities and difficulties of portfolio or contingent working (Handy, 1994: Feldman, 2006) and the uncertainty and disillusion faced by adult educators as they contemplate the future. Career identity refers here to the ways in which adult educators define and re-define themselves as practitioners, make meaning of their work and envisage their working futures (Ball and Goodson, 1985; Epstein, 1978; Hodkinson and Sparkes, 1997; Sachs, 2003; Lasky, 2005; Ecclestone, 2007; Kirk and Wall, 2011).

As Figure 6.1 suggests, an individual's career identity may include personal and social factors arising from past experiences (family, education and previous work background), the present context for practice (the political and economic climate, workplace norms and

Figure 6.1 Factors influencing career identity

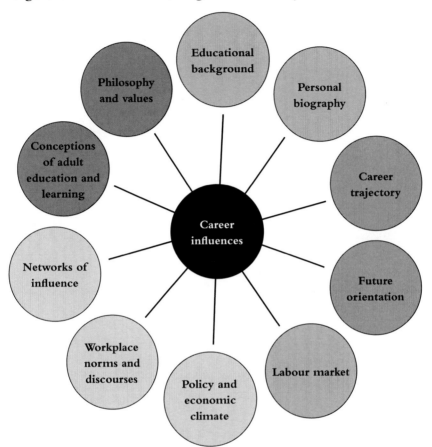

discourses) or envisaged futures (which may involve consideration of job opportunities, promotion, redundancy or retirement). Career identity is also influenced by an individual's values and beliefs about the nature and purposes of adult education. Careers are therefore shaped by structural factors, by political and economic climates and by subjective values, dispositions and biographies (Ball and Goodson, 1985; Hodkinson and Sparkes, 1997; Kirk and Wall, 2011). Like the term 'career', the concept of a career trajectory might once have implied a fairly straightforward progression from 'launch' to 'landing' (Huberman, 1995). It is doubtful that this has ever been the case for teachers of adults, who are likely to come to teaching late in life and whose work might be hourly-paid or run alongside other commitments. The concept of career trajectory here is used descriptively to refer to past, present and contemplated future work roles, influenced both by external factors and those specific to the individual, including their aspirations and desires.

Six portraits of a career in adult education

This section describes the careers of adult educators through the narratives of six interviewees who were at different stages in their working lives, three from New Zealand and three from England. The portraits illustrate how, typically, adult educators enter the field, the qualification routes they take, the value they place on their work and their view of their career prospects. I begin with a brief pen picture of each adult educator.

Portrait one: Moira, England, full-time community adult educator, five years

Moira studied art at university and wanted to be a professional artist. In the meantime she had combined a number of part-time jobs, including teaching A-level media studies and care work. Having gained a full-time job in a care home she temporarily abandoned teaching. She eventually returned to part-time adult teaching and at this point gained a teaching certificate. She then studied for a Master's degree in photography. Moira was offered work with a local education authority, teaching drama and digital photography. As cuts began to bite, she moved from this role to become a lead tutor with another authority. Although her job was relatively secure at the time of the interview, she was concerned about the future.

Portrait two: Karen, New Zealand, part-time adult educator and volunteer, six years

Karen had trained and worked as a primary school teacher. However, when she and her family moved to a new town she gained employment as a school-based ACE co-ordinator. This part-time job was one aspect of her wider voluntary involvement in community education activities. Karen had recently been made redundant following government cutbacks to ACE provision in schools. She now teaches an art-based leisure class at her local college on an hourly-paid basis and continues to work as a volunteer in her community.

Portrait three: Alex, England, full-time college-based adult educator, 11 years

Alex had been a mature student at a residential adult education college. He had gone on from college to study for a degree in social science and a postgraduate certificate in post-compulsory education (PGCE). Because he had been keen to combine travel and paid work he also studied for a qualification to teach English as foreign language. He gained part-time work in a college, teaching sociology on an access to higher education course but he needed full-time work to support his family. Eventually he gained full-time employment as a resident tutor at the college where he had himself been a student. Over time, he took on more of a teaching role at the college and became a full-time, permanently employed social sciences teacher. However, in the light of changing policy in post-compulsory education he felt that his future prospects as a teacher of a non-vocational subject were far from secure.

Portrait four: Debbie, New Zealand, part-time ESOL tutor, 12 years

Debbie worked as a literacy and language teacher with migrant learners in a community setting. Her specialist focus was 'pre-literate learners' who tended to be older women or people with disabilities. She began as a volunteer and slowly picked up more paid work over the years. Debbie had a degree in social sciences but when she began teaching she did not have a teaching qualification. She therefore studied part-time at her local polytechnic, gaining a certificate in adult teaching and a graduate diploma in teaching ESOL. Debbie was becoming frustrated by funding constraints and lack of professional recognition. At the time of the interview she was deciding whether to give up adult education work.

Portrait five: Carla, England, part-time adult educator and volunteer, 30 years plus

Carla's teaching areas included IT, history, philosophy, science and politics. She also taught on a further education teachers' certificate course. She had worked for a range of employers in the voluntary, local government and college sectors – frequently in more than one job at any one time. She had a Bachelor's degree and was a qualified teacher of adults. She held local and national roles representing the interests of adult educators. The variety of hourly paid jobs on which she relied had progressively been reducing. She had gone from working five days to less than six hours a week. At the same time she could not afford to retrain: she was in a 'qualifications trap' as a result of government regulations which had withdrawn fee subsidies from people already holding higher level or professional qualifications.

Portrait six: Imogen, New Zealand, part-time adult educator and volunteer, 30 years plus

Imogen's involvement in adult education dated back to her childhood in Italy where lifelong learning had been embedded in the everyday activities of work and community life. She had not planned to become a teacher, but she began teaching English on a voluntary, and then on a part-time paid, basis and she trained to become a teacher of English as a foreign language. It was a means of supporting herself while she pursued her ambition to travel.

Imogen taught English in Europe and Asia and eventually settled in New Zealand. She began teaching Italian privately to small groups. She also linked up with the Workers' Educational Association. Imogen's career was one of hourly-paid or casual contracts and voluntary work in a variety of adult education settings. For some years she managed the tension between a philosophical commitment to a non-institutional approach to adult education and earning a living. However, policy and funding changes increasingly restricted the opportunities for work. As cuts to ACE funding began to bite, opportunities to teach on a paid basis had almost entirely dried up and Imogen was reflecting on the course of what she described as her 'non-career'.

Routes to a 'non-career'

Hodkinson and Sparkes (1997) critique past theories of career choice (Krumboltz, 1979; Super, 1980; Kidd, 1984) for their tendency to over-emphasise the technical and rational nature of career decisions and to under-emphasise social and cultural opportunities and constraints. They identify individuals' decision-making as being determined by wider social, political, economic and cultural contexts in interaction with the individual and immediate concerns of people's lives. These may include personal preferences, unforeseen circumstances and desired futures. They may also include an element of chance. Each individual's horizon for action will therefore be differently determined, while also being structured by wider social realities. However, some common themes are identifiable in the narratives of adult educators in this study, which are illustrated in the six portraits presented in this chapter. The first is the haphazard nature of the choice of adult education as a career; the second is the attraction of adult education as a 'fall-back' career for those whose horizons for action involve an element of risk or uncertainty; the third is the association of adult education work with social and community purpose.

'Falling in' to adult education

Few of those interviewed appeared to have entered adult teaching through the kind of planned route generally associated with school teaching. Alex's 'I fell into it!' was illustrative of remarks made by a number of others, and has been noted elsewhere (Jephcote and Salisbury, 2009; Osborne and Sankey, 2009). Alex, one of the few of those interviewed who was in a permanent, full-time post, became an adult educator almost by default after he had gained his social science degree:

> I couldn't afford to do a Master's degree, so a PGCE was the alternative... I wasn't fed up with education after I got my degree, but I didn't get a good enough degree to be paid to do a Masters. I had two young children and so I thought, I need to get some training under my belt, a profession... So I thought, I'm not bored with education, I can still get a grant to do a PGCE and my mum was on my back saying you'd better get something out of this degree.

However, he also linked his career choice with his own biography – returning to education later in life after a less-than-successful school experience, followed by spells of unemployment. Being an adult returner to education and a mature entrant to higher education gave him contacts in and experience of adult education, which eased his entry to a career. Like a number of others, he was also attracted by the transferability of adult education qualifications to other contexts. The idea of training as a foreign language teacher suited Alex's aim to earn money while travelling.

Similarly, Imogen, who described her 30 years as a teacher of adults

103

as a 'non–career' had seen the potential value of training as a teacher of English as a foreign language as a means to combine work and international travel which eventually brought her from Europe to New Zealand:

> *I never wanted to be a teacher because my mother was a teacher. I was going to be a journalist or a public servant and I secretly always wanted to write but I felt that was a self-indulgent thing that rich people do when they've got spare time… But I started working with adult groups, ESOL groups in the UK. I worked as a volunteer and did a little bit of paid work for a community language centre. That was because I wanted to travel.*

The casual nature of much adult education work (particularly in the field of language and literacy teaching) means that paid work opportunities may emerge as a result of, or in addition to, unremunerated voluntary work. This reflects the historical position of adult education whose activities have had a marginal status in public policy. The idea of a skilled teacher not being paid for providing educational opportunities would be unlikely to be well received in school-based education. It is widely accepted in adult education.

A 'fall–back' career

Combining paid work with overseas travel is one reason why an individual might see adult education as a positive career choice. Another is its flexibility for individuals whose ultimate career aspirations entail a degree of risk and uncertainty. For example, it could be used to advantage by graduates whose personal aims require a fall-back position. It had made practical sense to Moira, an artist, who had been looking for paid work which did not compromise her main career aim:

> *I thought that teaching was a good way to combine being a practising artist and being able to earn money to live.*

It was also a part-time option for professionally qualified women wishing to re-enter the labour market and combine work with care commitments, like Debbie, who had to give up full-time work as a librarian when one of her children became ill. In adult literacy and language education it has been common for teaching roles to be performed on a voluntary or hourly-paid basis by women combining work with childcare responsibilities. In this sense, adult education is gendered work. Women's over-representation in part-time and hourly paid roles appears to have changed little since 1997 when Jane Thompson, writing of the situation in England, noted:

> *Women constitute the majority of volunteer tutors in literacy,*
> *adult basic education and English as a second language schemes.*
> *They are also more likely than men to be part-time tutors in local*
> *authority provision. As such they have little influence, receive*
> *low rates of pay, and enjoy no recognisable career structure except*
> *as token women in an essentially male-dominated profession.*
> (Thompson 1997: 45)

Little surprise then, perhaps, that adult educators have enjoyed limited success in winning improved remuneration and employment conditions.

A career with a social mission

For a sizable proportion of those interviewed, the idea of a career as an adult educator was explicitly value-driven. In New Zealand, in particular, paid work was often only one aspect of the community activity undertaken by adult educators. This seems to reflect the strongly networked nature of some communities in New Zealand, particularly in rural and semi-rural settings. Karen's profile illustrates this. She describes her activist motivations which coincided with her need for a job:

> *I have always been interested and involved with people of all ages.*
> *We shifted to a new town... There was quite an extensive ACE*
> *programme, but I could see how it could be done better. When the job*
> *came up, I applied. My background also includes a stint as chair of*
> *another college community education committee as a trustee. So there*
> *has been an interest for a long time.*

Similarly, Debbie linked her career choice with her personal experience and she took up unpaid adult education work, initially out of a commitment to promote literacy and language learning:

> *I have always been interested in reading and writing. Over my life*
> *I have met many local people who went through the school system*

*and came out the other side unable to read and write well or almost
not at all. My husband was severely dyslexic and unable to read until
aged 30… Our grandson is also severely dyslexic and sadly has had
very little sensible help through the school system… I guess that was
one motivation. My second motivation was my interest in the arrival
of refugees from Somalia and Ethiopia in my home city about 15
years ago. I wanted to meet them.*

Carla's motivation was borne of a commitment to education for
democracy. She had chosen to work as an adult educator to sustain a
career identity which was congruent with her beliefs:

*I am very passionate about education; it's welded into virtually
everything I do. In many respects I'm like a lot of part-timers
and contractual people working in the business, I did it because
I wanted to do it; because I was enthusiastic about it. It changes
people's lives.*

The sense of social mission was a recurring theme. Not only was it common for these adult educators to work well beyond the terms of their
paid contracts; participation in voluntary work or in outside paid work
was also commonplace. This suggests some continuity between adult
educators' sense of their own teacher identities and their public, community and personal identities. However, this is not recognised in their
social status, their conditions of work or in the way they are positioned
by policy discourses of professionalisation.

The double-edged sword of non-standard career routes

It is difficult to imagine adult education being proposed as a career
pathway for a young person planning their future. Because there is no
clear way in, there is a tendency for people to 'fall' in. Career decisions
combine pragmatism and idealism. On the one hand, the philosophical
underpinnings of adult education – radical or liberal/humanistic – have
attracted people whose perspectives on education were as likely to be
driven by public service ideals as by career aspirations. Adult education's
connection with the idea of a reforming or ameliorating 'mission' has
meant that those who choose to work within it have seen their work
as intrinsically important, over and above financial reward. This has

made their exploitation as workers relatively easy. The strength of social and emotional commitment to adult education, particularly among longstanding adult educators whose entry to the field coincided with a more radical period in adult education's history, has challenged their educator identities as their status and working conditions have worsened. On the other hand, the flexibility of a career in adult education work has been useful for combining work with other commitments and aspirations. In this sense, the casual nature of adult education work may have been used to advantage. However, this has reinforced its low status and helps to account for its relative lack of worker organisation. Both motivations tend to work against the prospects for job security and a level of remuneration which reflects the level of expertise required.

Qualification pathways

If the reasons for entering a career in adult education are varied, qualification pathways are equally so. There has traditionally been no single qualification route to teaching in adult education and, in England in particular, qualifications have been subject to a good deal of change, as discussed in Chapter Three. Recent attempts to impose a qualifications framework on workers in post-compulsory education in England have been only partially successful – and least successful of all in the adult and community learning sector (BIS, 2012b,c)

Most of the adult educators interviewed in the course of the research for this book had subject-specialist undergraduate and postgraduate qualifications; most also possessed teaching, social work, management or other professional credentials. Of the 62 adult educators interviewed, almost all held a Bachelor's degree or a teaching qualification. Most held both a degree and a professional qualification in teaching or a related professional area. A number held multiple qualifications – in their subject area and in teaching (see Table 6.1).

Of the six adult educators whose narratives are recorded in this chapter, all were qualified to teach: Alex, Moira and Carla in England were qualified teachers of adults and in New Zealand Imogen was qualified as a TEFL teacher, Karen was a trained primary school teacher and Debbie was qualified as a teacher of adults and in teaching English to speakers of other languages. The picture which emerges is one of multiple qualifications acquired through a desire to increase

Table 6.1 Qualifications held by adult educators interviewed

	New Zealand	England
Bachelor's degree	25	28
Master's degree	5	7
Doctorate	2	4
School teaching qualification	10	3
Adult teaching qualification	9	20
ESOL/TEFL qualification	6	8
Other professional qualification	6	2

knowledge and improve practice, rather than through prescription. Moira explains:

> *I began by doing a PTLLS [Preparing to Teach in the Lifelong Learning Sector] certificate just so I could teach adults in 2007. I realised I would rather go down the academic route thereafter and I completed my postgraduate certificate in post-compulsory education in 2009. Not long after this I completed my QTLS [Qualified Teacher Learning and Skills]. I immediately followed this by doing a Master's degree in digital photography at university. I am still studying for this and should be completed in 2012 and hope to continue on to a PhD.*

As we saw in Chapter Three, professional development and training in England and New Zealand have been central to debates about the funding of adult education. However, the evidence here suggests that adult educators are not lacking in education or training; indeed they seek it out, though their efforts to do so may be frustrated. In Carla's case, the UK government's denial of subsidy for studies at a level equivalent to or lower than that already achieved (the 'ELQ' – equivalent or lower qualification regulation) meant that she 'could not retrain when her teaching work began to dry up.

> *I'm trying desperately to retrain, which I have found difficult to do. I'm caught in the qualification and funding trap. I already have a degree, so I can't retrain at the same level without paying enormously high fees which I can't afford. As somebody who has already got a*

degree I can't apply for a loan to get another degree... In effect, I'm locked out of progression, expanding my dimensions, because there isn't the opportunity there – the support for people with low incomes even though their qualification might be quite high level. I can't move in either direction.

The level of training and qualifications evident among this group of adult educators gives the lie to their characterisation, in both England and New Zealand, as workers in need of professional development. At the same time opportunities to study adult education theory and practice at higher levels are becoming fewer in both countries and the policy focus has been on lower level training and professional development.

Contingent careers

The patterns of tenure for the adult educators interviewed for this book are indicated in Table 6.2.

Table 6.2 Patterns of tenure for adult educators interviewed

		New Zealand	England
Full-time contract	Male	1	6
	Female	6	13
Part-time single contract	Male	0	0
	Female	6	4
Multiple contracts	Male	2	0
	Female	12	7
Volunteer	Male	1	0
	Female	3	0
Retired	Male	0	1
	Female	0	0

It was difficult to identify full-time adult educators in New Zealand, apart from those working in larger national organisations. At the time of the interviews, cuts to school- and university-based adult education had further reduced the number of full-time and fractional contracts. In England, full-time adult educators were employed in local authority community education departments and in further education colleges, as well as in national organisations although, at the time these interviews were conducted, those in local authority employment were at risk from government cuts in local funding.

Around half those interviewed held part-time jobs. These were characteristically paid by the face-to-face teaching hour – often without preparation time included. Some adult educators combined paid part-time work with voluntary work, or paid contracts with self-employment. Some were formally 'retired' but taught a few hours a week. A sizable proportion of those interviewed held multiple, variable contracts – they were what Handy (1994) has described as portfolio workers and what others have called 'contingent' employees (Feldman, 2006; Redpath *et al.*, 2009). Contingent employment is a growing global trend; it has become increasingly common among higher-skilled workers (Redpath *et al.*, 2009), though arguably it has long been a feature of adult education work. Its defining characteristics include less-than-full-time engagement with more than one employer and contracts of limited or unpredictable duration.

Carla, in England, and Imogen, in New Zealand, were contingent workers of long standing. Their career patterns were strikingly similar. Both had worked in universities and colleges, for the WEA and community-based organisations on multiple casual contracts in their respective countries, as Carla explains:

> *I've done stuff in further education and I have done quite a lot of stuff in higher education as well. But these areas do overlap on a regular basis. I'm a contractual tutor who does these things on a whenever-it's-possible basis… I've worked for pretty well every organisation you can think of, including a lot you have probably never heard of.*

Similarly, Imogen described her non-institutional orientation and her commitment to creating learning opportunities as much as to earning a living:

> *The way I chose to work was making decisions based on what they call kaupapa.* By definition that's really the opposite of looking*

---

* Principles and ideas informed by a Māori world view.

110

*for a job in an institution and then working for the institution. I've
had a terrific amount of involvement – working with, working for,
working on projects, being involved in meetings with people who
work in institutions. And I can see that the focus is often totally
different; you're serving the institution and it's called adult education,
or community education; those are the names that are given but the
reality is that it is an institutional function, you have constraints and
it's not to do with meeting learning needs, but it's to do with meeting
the institution's needs.*

As well as working on hourly-paid contracts and as a volunteer WEA
committee member, Imogen had brought small groups of people
together who shared a common interest in language learning, running
classes in private homes and charging the group just enough for her
to make a small profit, or joining up with local organisations to set up
classes on a shoestring.

The other aspect of adult educators' contingent careers was that their
commitment often extended well beyond what they were paid for.
Again, this had both positive and negative implications for a part-time,
community-based worker like Debbie:

*I have never worked in an institutional educational setting which
means I work harder and am paid less than my contemporaries, but
also have had more freedom in how/what I teach, less emphasis on
assessment (pass/fail) and a much more holistic approach to learners.*

This was not only the case for part-time workers – indeed it will be a
familiar story for people working across all sectors of education. Moira
described the hours of unpaid work she undertook at home and the
impact of monitoring regimes on creative adult education:

*... there is a lot more paperwork in order to 'prove' that you do a lot
of things. For instance to prove that you differentiate, that you are
embedding key skills, that you have used sustainability, that you have
set goals. All of these things now have to be shown and evidenced...
I think that evidencing to an extent is needed but it does mean that
all the creativity can be sucked right out of you in order to ensure that
you have done other things!... I also think that teachers are leaving
the teaching profession as they are expected to do a lot more for a lot*

less. I do a lot of work at home for my job, most of which is basically unpaid and so do many other teachers and this is why good teachers give up.

Karen's profile, too, illustrates the casualised and temporary nature of adult education work in New Zealand. At the time she was interviewed, the cuts to school-based adult education in New Zealand had just begun make their impact felt and many schools were withdrawing altogether from their involvement in ACE.

Having been suddenly widowed with two dependants, and then losing my ACE job, I have continued to work voluntarily in my local community. I sit on the Ministry of Social Development's community response forum… I am a trustee for the Arts Centre and I'm currently working on designing an arts education programme there in conjunction with a small group of others… Very exciting! All this is voluntary and I'm also seeking paid employment.

While not all those interviewed were contingent employees, there was a strong tendency for this to be the case, particularly for women. Contingent employment has considerable advantages for the employer – it is easier to control costs and avoids the need to factor in holidays, staff development and training. For some workers too, it offers a degree of autonomy and challenge. However, as Redpath *et al.* (2009) have suggested, contingent employment brings with it psychological uncertainty as well as negative effects on future career prospects.

Contemplating the future: Career prospects in adult education

Looking at the data overall, it is first worth noting that of the 62 people interviewed for this research, just under one third had already experienced redundancy or reduced working hours, had recently retired or were planning to leave publicly-funded adult education altogether – a stark indication of the problems faced for adult educators considering their future careers. The attitudes to the future of those remaining in employment ranged from resigned pessimism to desperation. Although in permanent full-time employment, Alex was aware that dedicated college-based work with mature students was at risk:

112

*I think the problem is that the government are killing the whole
access movement off with the idea that they are not going to fund
over-25s. As far as I can see, education, you either pay for it yourself
or forget it. Most people coming from poorer backgrounds are not
going to have the money… If the changes come in, then our access
course has got another year and it's finished.*

In the meantime he was prepared to hold on and adjust to changing
policy circumstances. Debbie too, had concluded that uncertainty and
insecurity were the price to be paid for working 'on the margins' of
education. However, she was reaching the limits of her own ability to
endure:

*… I have come to accept that this work will never be properly funded
and those of us who work on the outer edge of the profession will not
be respected in what we do as we are seen as not fully professional.
Also, as our students are marginal people, our role is seen as being of
marginal importance. However, that all doesn't really worry me that
much as I have always felt comfortable on the margins because that
is where creativity and innovation flourish… Unfortunately after
12 years I'm tired and broke and I feel my time is nearly up in this
job…*

Of the six adult educators whose narratives are related in this chapter,
Carla and Imogen – whose careers were longest, whose commitment
was the most strongly expressed in social terms and who had been most
dependent on multiple contracts with multiple employers – were both
close to despair. Imogen described the collapse of her WEA classes with
the loss of ACE funding in New Zealand. Likewise, Carla had lost her
WEA teaching and much of her other work:

*Two years ago I would have been teaching five days a week for
four-and-a-half hours a day contact time; and three nights and
occasional weekend day schools. Although it wasn't a huge income,
it was enough to keep me going. Now it has shrunk to about six
hours a week. It's a huge drop. Every so often I'll get letters from my
employers saying we're facing redundancies, we don't know what's
going to happen next. It has become a very scary thing to be involved
in… For many of us in adult education, we had faith in it; faith in*

its redeeming quality in human society and its capacity to change people; we still do thoroughly believe in that. I know many tutors who signed up to that manifesto and predicated their lives upon it. The blow of the shrinkage is not necessarily just the lack of income. It's the shock to self-esteem and the identity that goes with it.

And, ironically, at the same time as she was losing most of her part-time hours of teaching work, she was being required to pay to register as a member of her professional body – the Institute for Learning – as a condition of remaining an adult educator.

Summary: A career in adult education?

Flexible capitalism has blocked the straight roadway of career, diverting employees suddenly from one kind of work into another. The word 'job' in English of the fourteenth century meant a lump or piece of something which could be carted around. Flexibility today brings back this arcane sense of the job, as people do lumps of labour, pieces of work, over the course of a lifetime. (Sennett, 1998: 9)

What does it mean to try to make a working life in adult education? If adult education was always on the margins of public education provision what prospects are there for those who have carved out careers in this field? The six portraits above reveal striking similarities between the career experiences of English and New Zealand adult educators. They are portraits of committed, adventurous, experienced and educationally well-qualified people. While these adult educators may have fallen somewhat haphazardly into their careers, they had knowledge and skills and espoused values which, in other contexts, would be associated with professionalism – and a sense of vocation expressed through the notion of working for the public good. In both countries, however, the idea of a career – or even a job – in adult education is problematic. It will almost certainly be characterised by insecurity, poor working conditions and poor pay and it may well end in despondency. The strength of social and emotional commitment to adult education, particularly among longstanding adult educators, whose entry to the field coincided with a more radical period in adult education's history, has left them in despair as their working conditions have worsened and their prospects have become more insecure. The policy rhetoric of lifelong learning has done nothing to alter this situation. The low status of adult education as a field of work clearly reflects the continuing low status of non-formal, adult-focused education. It is linked, too, to the relative weakness of their industrial organisation and the gendered nature of adult education work below the level of management.

CHAPTER SEVEN

Confronting the dilemmas:
Accommodation and resistance

*... we may be in danger of becoming the compliant purveyors of
'merely useful knowledge' (i.e. knowledge that is constructed to make
people productive, profitable and quiescent workers) as distinct from
the active agents of 'really useful knowledge' (i.e. knowledge that is
calculated to enable people to become critical, autonomous and – if
necessary – dissenting citizens).* (Martin, 2008)

*How do I survive otherwise in a world that isn't really supportive of
adult education?* (Gina, New Zealand, part-time adult educator,
25 years)

Introduction

How do adult educators manage the contradictions between their
beliefs about adult education and the expectations placed upon them by
policy? Do they feel obliged to accept without question the changing
requirements on their practice? Or are they able to draw on their values,
experience and the opportunities and resources which present themselves
(Biesta and Tedder, 2007) to resist imposed regimes of adult education
practice? This chapter explores the ways in which adult educators saw
themselves as exercising agency (Emirbayer and Mische, 1998; Biesta
and Tedder, 2007; Lawy and Tedder, 2009), working with or against the
thrust of policies and practices which they felt were not consistent with
their values as adult educators. Through the stories of four longstanding

adult educators it describes responses of accommodation or resistance. It discusses how these different responses were linked to practitioners' past experience, their philosophical theoretical underpinnings, their assessment of the possibilities for manoeuvre within their work context and their view of the future prospects. It suggests that the line between accommodation and resistance is not always easy to discern and that micro resistances are likely to be difficult to police, particularly for those who are newer to the field or whose practice is not firmly underpinned by theory.

Professional agency in practice

As adult education policy becomes increasingly commodified and dominated by instrumentalism, educators whose practice is informed by philosophical perspectives at odds with the global policy hegemony are likely to face conflicts between the expectations placed upon them and their own conceptions of good practice. Below I explore the extent to which it was possible for adult educators to exercise agency, finding space to work against the grain of policy. The term 'agency' is defined here as a process of engagement with a context in which practitioners – influenced by their experience, beliefs and aspirations – interact with the external demands made upon them (Emirbeyer and Mische, 1998; Biesta and Tedder, 2007; Lawy and Tedder, 2009) and make decisions about the possibilities and limits of action within that context. Agency, construed thus, is:

> ...not some kind of 'power' that individuals possess and can utilise in any situation they encounter. Agency should rather be understood as something that has to be achieved in and through engagement with particular temporal-relational contexts-for-action. Agency, in other words, is not something that people have; it is something that people do. (Biesta and Tedder, 2007: 136)

Emirbeyer and Mische (1998: 971) suggest three elements which constitute agency. First, the iterational element, through which actors draw on past ideas and experiences to sustain their sense of identity. In relation to adult educators' work, these might include values and beliefs engendered earlier in their lives or careers, past education and work experiences, as well as understandings developed with professional peers.

117

Second, the projective element, through which actors imagine future possibilities for action. In relation to the current discussion this might include an assessment of the possible outcomes of compliance, resistance or other forms of response to constraints or consideration of future career options or retirement. Third, the practice-evaluative element, as described by Emirbeyer and Mische, refers to actors' capacity to make judgements in response to demands emerging in their immediate practice context and how they deal with day-to-day dynamics of work with learners, colleagues and managers. While all three elements may be present within any instance of professional practice, Emirbeyer and Mische suggest that there may be conflicts between them and, importantly, that one or other element may dominate. The utility of analysing the perspectives of experienced adult educators against this tripartite conceptualisation of agency is that it enables us to discern the relative influence of past experience and values on practitioners' ability to act in a climate hostile to their beliefs about adult education.

Adult educators' perspectives on changing policy climates: Four portraits

Below I provide a pen picture of four experienced adult educators' career trajectories, their descriptions of their beliefs and values concerning adult education, the dilemmas arising from conflicts between their beliefs and the expectations laid on them by neoliberal and managerialist policies and how they have tackled them. The data illustrate the impact of neoliberalism and managerialism in both England and New Zealand and the degree to which adult educators drew on Emirbeyer and Mische's three dimensions of agency – past, present and future – to accommodate or resist those policy directives that were not consistent with their beliefs.

English narrative 1: Parvin, full-time ESOL teacher, 25 years
Parvin grew up in the Middle East and was involved in voluntary community work from an early age. Her first degree was in architecture, but when she arrived in the UK she began working in community development. She took a Master's degree and trained as a teacher while working in a community college. Local government cutbacks caused her to move into ESOL teaching. It was the best option in the circumstances:

I must say, that wasn't the career option for me because I quite like informal education and the bottom up approach, rather than top down approach which ESOL always is. But nevertheless, I still was working with people and students and that was quite nice.

Parvin's philosophy was influenced by her past experience and study:

I think education has to be something quite broad and holistic and has to help people expand what they have gained, or are gaining in their personal experiences. And what basically empowers them to take control of their lives... I quite follow Paulo Freire's idea of education and I seem to be at ease with quite a lot of what that reflects in ESOL... although I think that goes against the grain of capitalism. There is always going to be a challenge between that sort of education and education for targets and so on.

She identified three challenges which conflicted with her view of adult education: the introduction of fees for ESOL students, the increase in targeting and monitoring and the dominance of instrumentalism:

In my view education should be entirely free... The other thing I think is the amount of paperwork; the tracking we have to do is very time consuming. It doesn't allow much time for preparation and for creativity... I think provisions are going to be streamlined to be target-driven and very much fitting with the economy, rather than people's development. And with that go all the problems of whether we will then have equal access for everyone. Unfortunately losers in this situation are not very obvious; they are voiceless people...

Parvin saw her long experience as enabling her to relax about the demands put upon her. She talked of herself as being able to 'work outside the box' and contrasted this with younger workers' reluctance to do so. She could also contemplate future work outside constraints in her retirement:

You learn how to be very flexible and explore and exploit opportunities when they are offered... I suppose – it's not easy, but I don't think I panic a lot... I am 60 this year and so I'm approaching retirement. Retirement, as far as I'm concerned,

*doesn't mean not working. I would very much like to perhaps look
at opportunities with UNICEF and places like that which will
allow me to do some project work in Farsi-speaking countries like
Afghanistan or Pakistan because I am bilingual.*

English narrative 2: Ursula, full-time community learning manager, 26 years

Ursula described having 'fallen into' adult education, though she also felt
there were 'personal political' motivations involved in her decision not
to teach English in a private language school. She began as a volunteer
ESOL teacher:

*It's a funny mixture of things in a way, because it's where I found
myself, but it's also driven by a political commitment to working with
people who are – in an unequal society – disadvantaged in many
ways.*

She had worked for over 20 years in the same organisation she had
started in as a volunteer:

*I started getting regular part-time work, became an ESOL lecturer; I
did a diploma in teaching English to speakers of other languages...
Then I was what was called a curriculum support worker. And then I
shifted over to family learning... I'm the family learning programme
manager now.*

Although Ursula's commitment to work with adult learners had been
based in social justice values, she had not consciously applied them until
recently, when she began a Master's course:

*Up to very recently I hadn't really thought about that at all.
I suppose the adult educator that recently I've read is Freire... I
thought that stepping back and looking at the theory of education
would be helpful, and it has been... it's been really interesting and
has given me a way of thinking about stuff that I was thinking about
already but maybe without knowing... particularly about citizenship
and social cohesion agendas and about: what are people learning to
do? Are we just teaching them to fit in to an unequal society?*

Ursula talked of dilemmas around monitoring and inspection:

> *There's a bit of conflict: there's all that evidence that you have to supply to funders to say that you're worth your money, and there's another body of evidence that you have to supply to [The Office for Standards in Education], which is completely different. And you have to have these two hats on; one is to do with quality and one is to do with quantity. And the equation for me doesn't always match up.*

'Stepping back' and looking at her current work through the eyes of theory was affecting how Ursula saw her practice:

> *I think it's beginning to feed back, in a way that is quite subtle. Some of the things are about resistances. I think there are small resistances you can make as an adult educator within your work. A lot of the time you are complying, but there are more things you can do. And ways that you can work, that you can feed in and challenge yourself a bit to think in new ways and see if you can bring it into your practice.*

She spoke of how she was able to challenge some of the expectations around measurable outcomes, prescribed curricula and instrumentalism in community-based education; she had also become alert to the danger of getting 'sucked in' by managerialist assumptions:

> *It's so easy when you are at a meeting with people, you get sucked into things and then you have to pause and think: hang on a minute; I'm getting pulled down here. You have to pause and regroup. I think I do that... It isn't all about jobs and it is actually about people's connection with the community they live or work in.*

Ursula drew on her developing theoretical understanding to check herself as a manager. She also drew on her age and experience to 'dodge and weave a bit' around guidelines:

> *You've got to have the confidence of your experience and the fact that you have been somewhere a long time, so nobody's going to do anything too terrible to you. You cross a few borders sometimes. I think it is harder for people that come into it now. I think it's easier*

for people like me who've been in it a long time and have experienced the different possibilities that have come and gone... To be honest, when I first started, I was obsessed with the guidelines as well. But with experience, you begin to think: Oh well I'm sure I could do this. That does come from that confidence of experience. New people coming in − seem to be so part of the neoliberal thing that there's no way of looking out of it. Whereas we − I don't know whether it's age or whatever − there's a way of seeing something different that some of the new people coming in don't seem to see.

New Zealand narrative 1: Gina, part-time adult educator, 25 years

Gina trained as a primary school teacher but after returning from working in Europe she was unable to find a job in that field. After a brief period as a care worker, she became a volunteer literacy teacher. Gina was motivated by a desire to broaden her horizons:

I felt like I had opportunity, not privilege − but it was a privilege in that I had an educated family. My parents were teachers; I had gone to teachers' college and I had a sense that it was a little bit narrow. So I wanted to broaden my middle class, white New Zealand background probably. It was me discovering myself as well.

She described her philosophical base as humanistic and her motivation to support personal growth and assertiveness, particularly among women:

It was more of a humanist, holistic approach. It was based in social justice and opportunity for all; facilitating learning to empower. Empowerment was a big thing for me, working with women who had been victims mostly and had no power.

Gina saw her role as a facilitator of group learning in the adult education classroom:

Using the skills of the group; using their experience and trying to make it enjoyable and relaxed. But obviously with a structure... So there is that balance... My approach is probably a bit gentle too. I don't want to make people feel uncomfortable.

She worked as an adult educator in custodial and community settings and was active in voluntary adult education. She gained a Master's in education and became an adult educator trainer. When teacher training colleges across New Zealand were merged with universities, her employment was transferred to the local university but within three years she was made redundant in the wake of cutbacks and restructurings which negatively affected university adult education:

> *I always thought we were vulnerable because we were marginalised, we were small. There was always that concern… And totally we weren't wrong there.*

After being made redundant Gina continued to work in adult education on part-time and casual contracts in private and voluntary sector organisations and at her local polytechnic and university. She also continued in a voluntary capacity. However, her paid work conflicted with her values around flexibility, informality and biculturalism:

> *When I think back… the community of practice we had, the events we had, the celebrations, the networking events; the fact that we felt a bicultural approach – learning together.*

She continued to try to work within a humanist philosophical framework but was finding it increasingly difficult:

> *It's an awful compromise of principles. But I think that's what has had to happen all the way along to survive as an adult educator. How do I survive otherwise in a world that isn't really supportive of adult education?… What else can you do? If I want to stay with what I love, I've got to make personal compromises. I'm doing a job and I'm thinking is this really helpful? What will this really mean and what will people gain? And what's the point?*

New Zealand narrative 2: Elaine, part-time co-ordinator, 20 years

Elaine was a school-based ACE co-ordinator. She had been a school teacher. However, after having children she decided to take part-time work in adult education; it enabled her to combine work and childcare.

She described her philosophy in the general context of lifelong learning:

> *To me it's just education – it's a lifelong journey, from the day they are born to the day they die. I wanted to make sure that once people left college, they still had opportunities to maintain lifelong learning, and at a reasonable cost.*

Her work had been subject to government funding cuts which had led many schools to close their ACE provision. Her school was committed to continuing but she now had to 'break even' financially at least. As a result, fees had gone up, some classes had been cut and Elaine was constantly looking for new ways to bring in fee-paying learners. She acknowledged the impact for some in her local community: 'Obviously it has knocked some people out because prices have had to go up.' In spite of this she remained quite optimistic about the prospects. 'I believe it will survive and rebuild here.' She felt that her willingness to adapt and innovate, coupled with the trust built with her school management over the years, would enable her to continue to offer educational opportunities:

> *With the change in policies, I've decided to make them work for me. There has been too much doom and gloom. This is what has happened, OK let's go with it and see how we can change it and make it really work. I have an incredibly supportive Board. Also, as I have been doing it for 20 years, I have a proven record. If it was someone coming in new who had only been doing it for a couple of years before the funding cuts, I can understand the Board being hesitant. We have a proven record here. It makes it easier to build up trust. I just have to make ends meet; it's not a money-making business. As long as I don't cost the School, then they are happy with the results. Because they believe in lifelong education and the other values that it has.*

Implementing neoliberal policies: some dilemmas for practice

These four narratives illustrate a disjunction between adult educator values – infused with humanist, radical and social justice beliefs – and the dominant policy discourses of marketisation and targeting. In

124

New Zealand, the impact of withdrawing subsidies from school and community-based adult education was still being worked out in practice. By 2012 many schools which had been major providers of adult education had closed their adult provision. Elaine's school, which had opted to continue to offer classes, was compelled to pass on to participants the full cost of all but a small number of targeted courses (in sign language, ESOL, literacy and numeracy). This led to the trebling of fees for some courses which, in turn, squeezed out lower income adults. At the same time, the take up of some of these subsidised courses was not strong. In order to make a profit she had to switch to offering only those courses that would attract the largest number of people and close courses that recruited fewer students. While this would make sense according to the 'logic of the market' it meant that language learning courses and courses around Māori arts and culture were unlikely to be viable. It also meant that the duration of courses had to be reduced to ensure that numbers were maintained over the year. In the case of language learning the 'logic of the market' meant that only short-run, beginners' courses were sustainable. Depth of learning was sacrificed to the need to maintain numbers. The changes Elaine described to her work as she strove to remain profitable without government subsidy revealed the contradiction between her 'lifelong learning for all' philosophy and the developing reality.

In both countries particular groups of adults (those with low quali-fication levels, literacy or language difficulties) were targeted as being in need of educational participation and therefore eligible for funding subsidy. In England targeting was invariably linked with the expectation that learners would reach prescribed and accredited levels of attainment. While the argument for targeting is that it increases educational oppor-tunities for people who most need them, it has a stigmatising effect, steering education towards individual remediation and away from the liberatory and socially cohesive aims which feature in adult educators' expressions of purpose. Adult educators in England were faced with the dilemma of trying to support the aspirations of adults most in need of education while their success was being defined, not by the learners, but by externally-imposed, credentialised outcomes. Their humanistic and social justice values confronted a narrow, mechanistic view of learner needs and achievements. Even where targets were linked to 'soft' outcomes (expressed qualitatively in terms of gains in confidence or the ability to undertake certain actions) these still carried assumptions about learners and their capabilities.

Also in England, auditing and inspection were sources of frustration arising from the contradiction between adult educators' desire to practice learner-centred pedagogy and the policy imperative which stipulated measureable outcomes as criteria for determining quality. In New Zealand, these regimes were less highly developed, although they were beginning to be felt in attempts to introduce specifications of what should constitute adult learner outcomes. However, non-accredited ACE was still recognised as being distinct from formal and accredited vocational education and training and had not been swept up to the same extent in the performative regimes of the polytechnics as were English adult educators.

While the particularities of policies were context-specific, there was a clear neoliberal thrust in the impact on adult educators' work. In both countries this gave rise to dissonances for workers whose values were articulated in terms of social justice or personal empowerment. And in both countries financial cutbacks had on impact on adult educators' fragile job security. The global neoliberalising project and accompanying managerialism presented adult educators with dilemmas which involved balancing their principles against job survival.

Adult educator agency: Accommodation and resistance

For the most part, adult educators in this study tried to maintain or push against the boundaries of the shrinking terrain of adult education. Most of those interviewed described how they creatively adapted or resisted policies which did not fit with their value positions. Below, I discuss how these four adult educators exercised professional agency (Emirbeyer and Mische, 1998), balancing their experience and values against the constraints of the context. Agency was most commonly articulated in two ways. The first is through accommodation, which was primarily present-oriented and focused on practical possibilities within the current context as a means of managing external pressures. The second is through micro-resistances, which drew on past experience and a value base articulated with reference to theory, to subvert or oppose external constraints.

Accommodation

As Elaine's narrative illustrates, some adult educators who remained in employment were still upbeat about the possibilities for the future. They regarded policy change as a fact of life to be negotiated in the here-and-now, anticipating that the situation would change with a future change in government. In the meantime, they felt it was still possible to find space for agency in the immediate context and to use this space to work for the benefit of learners and the community. Elaine attributed her room for manoeuvre to being a worker of long-standing who enjoyed a relationship of trust with her management. She was able to draw on their shared understandings, developed over 20 years, to give her a free hand in deciding how best to accommodate market principles within a lifelong learning ethos. Since the external policy pressures were largely financial and not, as in England, accompanied by prescriptions around accreditation and outcomes monitoring, she felt she could adapt within the context of an education marketplace. Her exercise of agency was specific to the immediate context, however, and therefore somewhat fragile. Furthermore, while she advocated lifelong learning for all, her orientation was pragmatic rather than ideological. Agency in this instance was a function of the interplay of past relationships, the hands-off nature of policy and management intervention in the practice context, and a view of the future which was premised on the maintenance of the local status quo and which did not look too far beyond the immediate context.

As Gina had found to her cost, a change in management or sudden policy turn might easily undermine the ability to accommodate to changing circumstances. In a different setting – university-based adult education – Gina had tried to adapt to a series of changes in her employment and her role. Her work role had been redefined and, in addition to teaching, she was expected to take on a research and consultancy role in order to generate more income. The courses she taught were, like Elaine's, shortened to ensure that they were profitable. She worked to new funding restrictions which changed the way in which she and her colleagues organised their courses and which diluted their bicultural ethos. Ultimately, her efforts to accommodate in order to survive were confounded by further organisational restructuring and she was made redundant. She had no option but to become a freelance trainer, working on short-term training contracts for private sector businesses and non-government agencies, which offered little space for her to adopt a humanist, holistic approach which promoted social justice and empowerment in the ways that she had aspired to. Her space for the exercise of agency through her paid work was almost completely constrained by the changes in her work context and the limited future prospects. The impact on her sense of identity and purpose as an educator was profound.

Resistance

Parvin and Ursula were illustrative of those adult educators who tried consciously to resist or subvert the intentions of neoliberal and managerialist policies. They described micro-resistances and creative adaptations of policy directives. Characterised as 'dodging and weaving' or 'working outside the box', these resistances involved finding ways to confound policy and funding rules without directly challenging them. Strategies of resistance within the classroom (for example, 'performing' in one way for inspections, and another in day-to-day relationships with learners) enabled more radically-oriented educators to feel that they were holding the space for critical pedagogy, encouraging learners to examine the injustices in their own lives. It also opened up the potential for resistive coalitions between learners and teachers outside the classroom, for example in the campaign against cuts in ESOL provision in England (Action for ESOL, 2012). At the level of programme organisation, creative adaptations quite often involved administrative sleight of hand – for example, re-naming courses so that learners could repeat qualifications they had failed and which had therefore made them ineligible for funding.

As both Parvin and Ursula suggest, this was likely to be easier for longstanding adult educators. Newer practitioners were seen as less likely to be able to draw on past experience to exercise agency in the classroom (Lawy and Tedder, 2009). Parvin and Ursula drew heavily on their past experience to push against restrictions. However, Ursula recognised that the line between 'small resistances' and tacit collusion was hard to self-police. Her ability to do so was strengthened, not just by experience, but also through returning to study which afforded opportunities for critical reflection. Ursula's sense of professional agency was thus influenced by the present context-for-action as well as the past. Parvin drew on both theory and experience through her connection with the past. But her sense of freedom from policy constraints was additionally shaped by the projective dimension – her knowledge that retirement from paid employment would free her to work in accordance with her principles.

Summary: Working in spaces – or 'living in the cracks'?

An optimistic view of how adult educators manage the contradictions between the expectations laid upon them by policy and their beliefs about the purpose of their work is offered by Coare (in Coare and Johnson (eds), 2003: 51). She suggested that they are adept at: '... working creatively in the spaces of government policy' harnessing opportunities for using funding and other resources in ways consistent with values of social justice. An earlier, more pessimistic view, offered by Thompson (in Mayo and Thompson, 1995: 2), was that adult educators have become disillusioned and intimidated to such an extent that:

> ... *the price paid for holding on to jobs, and even achieving*
> *promotion, had been widespread demoralisation and incorporation –*
> *in the original sense of the word.*

She concluded that, far from working creatively in spaces, practitioners saw themselves as having no option but to 'go along with the new order and live in the cracks'. The four narratives above demonstrate how long-standing adult educators saw themselves as exercising agency in their daily practice through mobilising their beliefs and experiences and their assessments of the room to manoeuvre.

Educators adopting tactics of accommodation made optimistic judgements about the present possibilities without a critical assessment of the potential future impact. Nor did they always address the conflict between espoused values and decisions about practice – which tended to work against values of equal access and lifelong learning opportunities for all. 'Making it work' for the sake of maintaining the status quo appeared to be 'working in the cracks' rather than finding 'creative space'. Ultimately it was likely to be an unsuccessful tactic beyond the short term. As Gina had already found, accommodations are prone to be swept aside by changes in local management, restructurings or policy shifts.

Micro resistances involved a degree of tactical manoeuvring to confound the intentions of policy. They enabled adult educators like Ursula and Parvin to retain provision which they felt served the interests of learners and was consistent with a commitment to social justice. However, as Ursula recognised, individual, creative approaches had their limitations. First, the confidence to work flexibly with prescriptive regulations is not evenly distributed. For those newer to the field, their present context-for-action and their perspectives on possibilities for the future are likely to be a dominant determinant of agency (Lawy and Teddar, 2009). They are less likely to have the experience or the confidence to resist policy prescriptions. Second, the line between passive resistance and collusion is a difficult one to tread. Furthermore, it is not always easy to distinguish the one from the other. There is the danger of inadvertent incorporation into the dominant policy, particularly for workers who find themselves directly responsible for the implementation of policy. Third, and crucially, without a critical analysis of the political and ideological basis of prescribed policies it is difficult for an individual or group to resist the pressure to conform. Micro-level resistance is not in itself a strategy for change. Indeed, it may perpetuate an illusion that working creatively 'in the spaces' between policy intentions and regimes of accountability can turn the political tide. But it demonstrates the commitment of adult educators to find ways of working consistent with their beliefs about education's purpose. It maintains morale. Most importantly, in an era during which progressive politics is searching for ways to re-express itself, it keeps alive the experiences of a previous political era as a reminder – not just for activists – that other possibilities besides the current hegemonic 'normality' have existed and can exist again.

The narratives invite questions for critical reflection: what is the strategic potential of resistances which are not visible beyond the immediate context? Are accommodations or micro-resistances sufficient without critical analysis of the ideological context within which adult education is currently being re-shaped? And – beyond retirement, redundancy or departure from the field of adult education – what are the projective and strategic possibilities through which adult educators might imagine a future for adult education?

The bigger picture: Strategy and advocacy

I think what goes around will come around; we've been round this circle once or twice before. And to a certain extent the good stuff will carry on whatever... Because we'll find a way I think. Calling it something else, selling it to politicians, finding other ways... But if you look at what happened with ESOL... There are a lot of people who supported that campaign who are not in adult learning, but are tangential or who use ESOL provision for their clients; you've got to do that. (Faith, England, full-time adult educator, 12 years)

Introduction

Chapter Eight discussed the extent to which adult educators felt able to exercise agency in their everyday practice. This chapter looks beyond the immediate work context to discuss some of the social implications of ideas and policies circulating nationally and globally and the strategies that adult educators and their organisations adopted in response. The interviews in both England and New Zealand suggested concerns about targeting in a climate of funding cutbacks. These concerns went beyond adult education, to connect with wider anxieties about the impact of policies which harden social divisions and differentiate between the 'deserving' and 'undeserving'. Three distinct, but not mutually exclusive, types of strategic response were apparent, each of which is demonstrated above in Faith's contribution.

One was a kind of policy fatalism which suggested that the possibilities for influencing the direction of policy were so limited that the best strategy was simply to carry on and wait until the policy tide turned.

A second type of response involved exploiting the potential for developing adult education in ways which aligned with, or levered off funding from, government, corporate or philanthropic sources. Social enterprise (Bourzaga and Defourny, 2001; Grant, 2008; Thompson, 2008; Kerlin, 2009; Abu-Saifan, 2012) has been widely promoted as a solution to the withdrawal of the state from areas of social provision, including adult education and training. I discuss what the evidence suggests about social enterprise as viable strategy for practitioners with a concern for social justice and equality of opportunity. I argue that issues of definition, emphasis and politics require critical analysis before it can be concluded that social enterprise truly does offer a 'third way' between the state and the market for adult education practice. Third were the advocacy and campaigning responses developed in England and New Zealand by adult educators and learners to influence policy and change the nature of the debate. I discuss the strengths and limitations of strategies of advocacy and campaigning with reference to adult educators' views and the literature of international development campaigning.

Counting the social costs of adult education policies

As intimated in the last chapter, concern was expressed by adult educators in both countries about the social costs of current policies on adult education and training. These concerns went beyond adult education itself and linked to political debates around social inclusion, equality of opportunity and immigration. An example of the wider implications of government policies in both countries developed around 'targeting'. On the face of it, targeting – prioritising educational resources towards particular under-represented groups or specific activities – is a policy which seems self-evidently benign in its aim to prioritise 'needs' in a constrained fiscal environment, as Melanie suggests:

> *At heart, I believe in need rather than want. So I'm for promoting*
> *the skills that help people in their lives, like gardening, like*
> *composting, like cooking. And I don't care much about whether you*
> *can learn Spanish or Chinese cooking. Because I think those are*
> *just luxuries… But if you've only got so much money, you go the*
> *skill development way.* (Melanie, New Zealand, full-time adult
> education manager, 20 years)

However, targeting policies in New Zealand were seen as reinforcing divisions between those who were the focus of educational interventions (particularly people with literacy, language or numeracy difficulties, the jobless and Māori and Pasifika adults) and those who were judged able to pay for their adult education. Such policies also tended to stereotype negatively the targets of adult educational provision, compromising adult educators' values regarding equal access and cultural and community cohesion:

> *One rather large policy change I see is that almost all government funded ACE focuses on Māori, Pasifika and immigrants. There appears to be an almost explicit assumption that if you do not fall into one of these categories you must be self-sufficient financially and already well-educated and not in need of further qualifications.* (Karen, New Zealand, part-time adult educator and volunteer, six years)

> *People doing ACE are now feeling labelled as having 'learning disabilities'; why are we doing this to our adult learners? Not everyone has a literacy problem, yet we are forced to label them because of government policy or make them pay!* (Hilary, New Zealand, part-time adult education co-ordinator, 17 years)

In England, punitive targeting of speakers of languages other than English was used to position migrants and refugees as 'undeserving' if they were not engaged in ESOL classes, with potentially catastrophic consequences for their eligibility for state benefits. Even as government funding was being cut back, ESOL teachers made redundant and restrictions placed on eligibility for free ESOL classes, the government was accusing migrants of failing to learn English. For example, in his June 2013 spending review speech, George Osborne, Chancellor of the Exchequer, took the opportunity (without recourse to any evidence) to imply that immigrants were unwilling to access English classes and therefore undeserving of state support:

> *From now on, if claimants don't speak English, they will have to attend language courses until they do. This is a reasonable requirement in this country. It will help people find work. But if you're not prepared to learn English, your benefits will be cut.* (George Osborne MP, June 2013)

Meanwhile he failed to mention the cuts and restrictions imposed on ESOL provision by his own government. In a country in which immigration policy is central to the struggles for power between parties from the centre to the right of the political spectrum, adult education was being implicated in politically-motivated attempts to project England as hostile to migrants, as a means to deter immigration and satisfy the prejudices of a section of the electorate. Concern about the tendency to use the word 'language' as a proxy for 'race' (Action on ESOL, 2012) was voiced by a number of ESOL teachers in England:

> *From my point of view, teaching ESOL, there's this terrible racist agenda. 'Why should we be paying for people who don't even belong here?' The future doesn't look good.* (Sue, England, full-time ESOL teacher, 25 years)

> *And now immigrants are being treated with apparent disdain by some politicians, as though they weren't really worth investing in. It is shameful. I am not optimistic about the opportunities.* (Rita, England, part-time ESOL teacher, eight years)

These developments in New Zealand and England were examples of policies which ran counter to values of equality and inclusion. They represented a retreat from an ideal of adult education for the social and cultural (as well as economic) good. Importantly too, they demonstrate that changes affecting adult education emanate from wider political projects, some of whose socially divisive consequences may be unintended, some apparently deliberate.

Policy fatalism: 'What goes around comes around'

One response to the situation was simply to wait in the hope that the political climate or the government in power would change and that this would revive the fortunes of adult education in the way Brian suggests had happened in the past:

> *The challenge is for the organisation to survive the situation... We are so small that it is not worth the political cost... that's pretty much how we survived the Thatcher era... I think we may get away with*

that again, and wait for better times… (Brian, England, full-time adult educator, 30 years plus)

This policy fatalism suggested a sense of powerlessness and lack of confidence in political contestation. A general election was imminent in New Zealand at the time these interviews took place. ACE in New Zealand had experienced a brief resurgence in policy support under the 1999–2008 Labour coalition governments – though not a significant increase in funding. Therefore it was reasonable for practitioners to assume that a change of government might signal a more favourable policy climate:

> *It's going to be interesting in the next two years; it's going to depend on this election…* (Gloria, New Zealand, adult educator, 30 years plus)

> *If National gets in, I wouldn't mind betting that constraints come in. It will also be interesting to see what will happen if Labour gets in; they have a more social agenda. I still think it comes down to money and – I was going to say priorities – but sometimes the money wipes out the priority. I can't untangle the politics really because you have a Party that goes in for three years and then the other one comes in and undermines everything that has been done and it's chop and change.* (Edith, New Zealand, part-time ESOL teacher, ten years)

> *… the education system is a political football. New brooms sweep clean constantly causing turmoil and change that often is not any kind of improvement… People who are migrants, refugees, criminals, school drop outs or whatever are the first to be penalised when money is tight.* (Debbie, New Zealand, part-time ESOL tutor, 12 years)

The belief that a Labour-led government might pursue a more 'social agenda' might have been misplaced. The record of the 1999–2008 Labour-led coalitions suggests that the neoliberal imperative was still dominant, notwithstanding some tinkering in the social arena (Zepke, 2009). In the event, however, a right wing National Party coalition was returned to power for a second time in 2011. The climate for adult education was further constrained and the government hardened its stance against supporting adult education for broader, social and non-instrumental purposes.

In England, the decline of adult education which began under the Thatcher government in the 1980s accelerated throughout the 17 years of a Labour government and continued with the election of a Conservative-led coalition in 2010. Nevertheless there was still a strand of opinion which took the view that a change in government at national level would alter the trajectory of policy and, furthermore, that policy is by nature cyclical:

> *What goes around comes around. We'll go back to where we've been... It will take a long time for the people who are not educators to realise the impact of what they are pushing through at the moment.* (Fiona, England, full-time adult educator, 15 years)

> *I am a believer in cycles really. I think it will just go round and back again.* (Denise, England, full-time adult education co-ordinator, 25 years)

This policy fatalism assumes sharper differences between the main political parties and their coalition partners than exist in reality. In fact there has been considerable policy consistency around education and training regardless of the avowed political persuasion of the government in power both within and between these two countries (Olssen *et al.*, 2004; S. Ball, 2008a). This suggests that policies are in fact products of political and economic projects operating at a global, as well as a national, level and that any assumption that a change of government signals a substantial change in emphasis may require rethinking.

'Third way' strategies: The lure of social enterprise

> *I am much more now into social enterprise and I think that's what we really have to think about: how we can have community-based enterprises, community-based organisations that can be self-supporting and not constantly at the behest of contestable funding like tertiary education.* (Jackie, New Zealand, part-time adult educator, 20 years)

136

The model I'm using is social entrepreneurship really. It's not a voluntary organisation, it's a social business. And I thought, yes, that's the style for the future. (Alan, England, retired adult educator, 30 years plus)

While the overall thrust of policy may be consistent between governments, there has been no shortage of short-term targeted projects on the part of governments, which come and go with the government in power. The belief that the prospects for influencing political change are limited may encourage practitioners to consider the funding possibilities arising from of-the-moment policy initiatives. Social enterprise was one such idea whose star was in the ascendant between 2010 and 2013.

Social enterprise ideas are influenced by 'third way' theories (Giddens, 1998, 2000, 2001) which sought to reconcile 'market fundamentalism' and 'Keynesian welfare compromise' (Giddens, 2001: 2). One plank of Gidden's third way argument was 'civic entrepreneurship' through which he envisaged groups would: 'generate creative and energetic strategies to help cope with social problems' (Giddens, 2001: 8). Third way politics, which have been promoted by social democratic-leaning administrations in the USA, Europe, Australia and New Zealand from the mid-1990s, aimed to promote 'social inclusion, pluralism, and democratic involvement within an active civil society that supports a market economy' (Codd, 2002: 32). The encouragement of social enterprises – businesses with social purpose – has been integral to the implementation of these ideas. However, definitions of social enterprise and the social entrepreneur are both vague and contested (Borzaga and Defourny, 2001; Thompson, 2008; Kerlin, 2009; Abu-Saifan, 2012).

In England the policy fondness for promoting social enterprise emerged under Tony Blair's 'New Labour' premiership from 1997 (Blair, 1998). Among the measures taken in pursuance of this idea was the establishment in 2001 of a Social Enterprise Unit, tasked with co-ordinating and supporting social enterprise initiatives on the part of third sector and non-profit organisations. Even with a change in government in 2010 an element of third way influence has remained under the Conservative Party's current leadership. The 'Big Society' was one of the big ideas of the Conservative election strategy in 2010; its avowed intention was to encourage citizens to assume a greater role in community support through voluntary effort and social enterprise (Pattie and Johnston, 2011; Corbett and Walker, 2012). It also, conveniently, provided a rationale for further state withdrawal from aspects of public sector provision through:

> ... *a less centralised state, greater community involvement in decision-making, and a greater role for voluntary activity, charities and the 'third sector' in the provision of services currently provided by the state.* (Pattie and Johnston, 2011: 405)

Among those activities aimed at encouraging Big Society entrepreneurialism was the launch of the Big Society Network (funded by government) and the Big Society Bank which was to be 'an important catalyst for growing the amount of private capital available to support our social entrepreneurs' (HM Government, 2011: 5) and which encouraged private capital to invest in new and developing social enterprises. Alongside this, Community Learning Trusts (BIS, 2012e) have been rolled out and piloted among selected adult and community learning organisations. These have a strong entrepreneurial flavour, demanding that 'Pound Plus' – evidence that additional income (for example, from fees and sales) or value (for example, from volunteer input) – be extracted from learning activities.

In New Zealand, social enterprises have been a part of the landscape for some time (Grant, 2008) although up to the present they have not been a focus of government policy. Nevertheless, where national government has shown an interest in social enterprise it has looked to the UK and Australia in particular for inspiration (Department for Internal Affairs, 2013; Office for the Community and Voluntary Sector, 2013). Grant (2008) identifies a number of aspects of New Zealand history, culture and politics which shape the nature of social enterprise in that country. Among these she cites the spirit of 'settler' ingenuity and community self-sufficiency, which are embedded in the country's colonial past. She also discusses the ways in which Māori iwi (tribes) and hapū (sub-tribes) have utilised financial settlements, in compensation for historic land appropriations by the former British colonists, in ways which combined business ventures with community benefit to Māori. Furthermore, she links the growth of social enterprises with the neoliberalising tendencies of governments from the 1980s onwards and in particular to the preference for contracting out public service provision (for example, the care of the elderly and the ambulance service) to non-government and non-profit organisations.

As a consequence, social enterprise in both countries is an idea in currency among adult educators as they seek alternatives in the face of government cutbacks and funding restrictions. Some of the practitioners who were interviewed for this book were considering establishing social enterprises that would meet social and education aims, while being financially self-sustaining. Social enterprises were proposed in respect of a range of areas including adult mentoring and career guidance, adult education in residential care settings and support for women entering employment. The idea of social entrepreneurship has an added attraction perhaps in that rhetorically it combines commitment, ingenuity and social purpose with a promise of self-sufficiency. This is well-illustrated in Abu-Saifan's definition which imbues the social entrepreneur with a heroic ethos:

> ... a mission driven individual who uses a set of entrepreneurial behaviours to deliver a social value to the less privileged, all through an entrepreneurially oriented entity that is financially independent, self-sufficient or sustainable. (Abu-Saifan, 2012: 25)

While appearing to stand outside the neoliberalising camp, it holds out the prospect of freedom from the vagaries of state policy and funding. However, it is fraught with ambiguities and contradictions.

First, social enterprises must generate funding, if not from public sources (which are increasingly constrained) then from philanthropic or corporate donors. The evidence from both England and New Zealand suggests that this is not as readily forthcoming as the rhetoric suggests. Given the reliance of many third sector organisations on government-derived contracts, it seems unlikely that either philanthropy or corporate goodwill could fill the gaps left in services by drastic public sector cutbacks (Pattie and Johnston, 2011). Certainly in New Zealand, the response of the corporate sector seems muted (Grant, 2008; Tindall Foundation, 2009), while in England it remains to be seen whether the Big Society Bank will attract the enthusiasm of social lenders. In the absence of large scale funding, raising income from those who benefit from services either through fees or sales is the only other option, which places adult educators in the contradictory position of applying 'user pays' policies to social provision – a move which demonstrably ran counter to the values of adult educators in both countries.

Second, as Pattie and Johnston (2011) have argued, a social enterprise approach operating in a free market environment is likely to favour the involvement of those with pre-existing resources – including those of time, money and social and cultural capital. Those most in need may be least likely to be able to draw on such resources to organise services. They may be less likely, too, to possess the levels of optimism and trust which are concomitant with community involvement. Rather, they are likely to be reliant on the goodwill of more affluent others – where it can be found. Since social enterprise solutions to social needs are unlikely to be sufficiently large scale or evenly distributed across society to meet the needs of diverse populations, it might be anticipated that provision will be inadequate.

Third, the optimum balance between the social justice quotient and profit in the social enterprise concept is unclear and rarely defined either in statements from government or in the intentions of the adult educators interviewed for this book. Nor is it clear what the balance should be between paid staff and volunteer effort, or indeed whether a role exists for paid workers in a social enterprise. Discussion of social enterprise solutions tends to omit details of standards of service, regulation of expectations or remuneration of providers.

The application of social enterprise ideas to the adult and community education sector is popularly advanced as the solution to cutbacks and uncertainties in adult education provision. However, a more critical view suggests that it may merely be a way of further cutting public sector provision and creating volunteers out of what would once have been paid and experienced adult educators, and result in a patchy and unstable pattern of provision. The rhetorical force of the language of social enterprise needs to be critiqued by informed analysis of the ideology underlying its promotion and by research into the consequences for equality of access and opportunity.

Advocacy and campaigning strategies

In both countries there were examples of advocacy and campaigning for recognition and funding for adult education. The term advocacy is used here to refer to activities – which may include campaigning, lobbying and education – by means of which organisations seek to influence policy and bring about change which is in the interests of adult learners and those who facilitate their learning (Anderson, 2000). In the main, advocating for adult education takes place at three levels in England and

140

New Zealand: in broad cross-sector alliances, in national membership-based organisations and in (sector or sub-sector) grass roots practitioner and learner campaigns. In New Zealand in particular, some advocacy work also takes place at international level, particularly through the Asia and South Pacific Association for Basic and Adult Education (ASPBAE).* Here, however, I focus on advocacy at the national level. I discuss the nature and types of advocacy and campaigning around adult education, and their strengths and limitations. In doing so I draw on the literature of international advocacy and campaigning (Edwards, 1993; Anderson, 2000; Chapman and Fisher, 2000; Leipold, 2000) which offers useful lessons for non-government organisations operating at a national level. I also use illustrative examples for the adult educator interviews.

Sector alliances

Sector alliances are coalitions between organisations which work together to identify shared areas of concern and action. They may focus solely on advocating to government or they may operate on a number of levels (for example, combining advocacy with government via lobbying and mobilising public opinion). They may adopt primarily 'insider' strategies (working with government agencies to influence change) or primarily 'outsider' strategies (campaigning against a particular government department or policy), or they may combine the two types of activity (Chapman and Fisher, 2000). They draw on their cross-sector strength to influence policy.

New Zealand: ACE Strategic Alliance

The ACE Strategic Alliance was formed in 2006 by senior representatives from eight national ACE-related organisations, including non-government organisations, polytechnics and universities. The aim of the Alliance was to collaborate to ensure that ACE issues were kept on the political agenda, and to lobby government on behalf of the sector. The Strategic Alliance has acted as a 'high-level' forum rather than a campaigning body and its activities have been largely confined to meetings and to the production of strategy documents. During 2010, the Strategic Alliance completed a draft discussion document *Real*

---

* ASPBAE is a regional association of over 200 organisational and individuals. It was established in 1964 and aims to promote lifelong adult education and learning for all. One of its priorities is policy advocacy, which involves research, monitoring, lobbying and promoting awareness in alliance with others.

Value: Investing in Ordinary People. Adult and Community Education in New Zealand: the next 10 years (ACE Sector Strategic Alliance, 2011) which was the focus of meetings with government representatives. The strategies identified in the discussion document are broadly in line with pre-2008, and to some extent post-2008, government policy on ACE:

- to improve provider engagement with target learner groups and facilitate learner pathways for those who need assistance
- to develop an effective infrastructure
- to develop provider and practitioner capability (ACE Sector Strategic Alliance, 2011: 9)

The strategy document focuses on structure, competence and capability rather than resourcing. It does not address the issue of cuts to sector funding or the remuneration and conditions of sector practitioners. In recent years, the Alliance's main focus has been on working with government to develop a stronger ACE infrastructure, through 'an outcomes-based funding framework with criteria that address the needs of communities' rather advocating directly for the sector and its practitioners.

England: CALL (Campaigning Alliance for Lifelong Learning)

CALL was launched in 2008 in response to the loss of 1.5 million places for adult learners across England as a consequence of government changes to adult education funding. CALL was a broad-based campaign whose subscribers included trade unions, colleges and community-based adult education providers, religious and campaigning groups, as well as individuals. It was based on founding principles which included:

- access to high quality education for all
- universal access to basic skills, ESOL and ICT
- the maintenance of local-authority-based adult education and learning for a range of purposes, including personal development
- the right to second chance education for adults
- fair reward and recognition of adult education practitioners
- the involvement of learners, educators and communities in decision-making.

While CALL was broadly supportive of the government's emphasis on training for skills and employment, it argued that this should not be the sole focus of funding for adult education. It advocated the benefits of more broadly focused adult education for family and community, and for creativity, culture, health and well-being. CALL's lobbying activities peaked during 2008 and 2009 and drew some response from government and an offer of meetings with the then Secretary of State for Education. However, this was the highpoint of CALL activities and it has had a low profile since the election of the Conservative-led coalition in 2010.

Sector alliances: Strengths and limitations

The strength of cross-sector alliances is in their capacity to mobilise high-level responses to government across a sector, while still freeing constituent organisations to make representations on their own behalf (Leipold, 2000). Together, larger organisations (for example, trades unions and national co-ordinating organisations) have access to resources to sustain advocacy efforts over time. Importantly, too, they can have access to 'back channels' – pre-existing relationships with politicians and government officials – which mean that they may be able to meet with, persuade or influence those who are close to government decision-making.

However, this closeness to government can be problematic. First, depending on the extent to which the strategic alliance is inclusive of grass roots opinion, there is a tendency for it to seem remote from the day-to-day issues of practice. This can be perceived negatively by practitioners, particularly where communication about the activities of the alliance is poor. Second, alliances may be compromised through over-identification with government agendas: people who meet regularly have a tendency to become close and their views convergent (Edwards, 1993). In turn, this can lead to practitioners feeling let down by the compromises made between strategic alliances and policy makers – or worse, to feel that the alliance is more motivated to collaborate with government than with those whose interests it purports to represent. Third, a strategic alliance may be unstable where there is competition for funding between the organisations involved (ibid.). At the end of the day, sectional interests may override sector interests in the race to pull in funding or 'put bums on seats'. These strengths and limitations are well summarised by one English adult educator interviewed for the research:

> ... it's what I refer to as a carrot and stick approach. On the one hand we do all this heavy, noisy stuff in the media, which causes a

lot of media attention, then we also have the back channels which say: OK, what's going on; let's talk... It bothers me a great deal that organisations are so worried about their own existence that they're frightened they might say something which threatens themselves and therefore they throw themselves into collaborative schemes of action with other bodies, in case they are undermining their short- or medium-term future... (Carla, England, part-time adult educator and volunteer, 30 years plus)

Issues of openness, independence and clarity of expectation therefore seem to be central to the credibility of strategic alliances as far as grass roots practitioners are concerned. This signals their need to look not just to influence policy but also to communicate with members of constituency organisations.

National membership organisations

National membership organisations in the sector promote adult education and lifelong learning as an area of practice, raise awareness of the value of adult and community education and encourage adult participation in education and training. They may do this through research, training, publications and conferences and through the provision of resources and support to adult education providers. ACE Aotearoa and NIACE (the National Institute of Adult Continuing Education) are the main membership organisations for the sector in New Zealand and England respectively. As such they fulfil an advocacy role.

New Zealand: ACE Aotearoa

Adult and Community Education (ACE) Aotearoa has a long history of advocating for the ACE sector. Until relatively recently ACE Aotearoa operated through a local branch structure, although some branches were more active than others. This structure was compromised during the period from 1999–2008 when the Tertiary Education Commission (TEC), under the Labour-led government, sought to bring some order and control to the sector by superimposing a system of regional ACE networks on the ACE Aotearoa branch structure. These government-funded networks which were to co-ordinate local provision and provide a focus for professional development activities tended to undermine the autonomy of regional ACE organisation (Bowl, 2011). TEC regional networks in turn went into decline after the reduction of funding to local

ACE organisations which followed the election of the National Party-led government in 2008. Formal contact between ACE Aotearoa and its local members is now mainly via its conferences – especially its Annual Conference – its web-based information and newsletters. It has also taken on responsibility for allocating government funding for professional development and collaborative activities to local ACE organisations and is to a considerable extent reliant for its financial survival on government contracts to undertake specific sector-wide activities (ACE Aotearoa, 2012). This places it in the position of being both an agent of government and a sector advocate. Its advocacy role is carried out in the context of its membership of the ACE Sector Strategic Alliance and its attempts to develop a dialogue with government ministers on policies which are relevant to adult and community education.

England: NIACE

NIACE is a well-established membership organisation which, *inter alia*, advocates for the adult and community learning sector, seeking to influence government and the wider public to support and increase opportunities for adults to engage in learning. It was a founding member of CALL. Much of its advocacy activity involves collecting and disseminating evidence around the value of lifelong learning. In 2007 NIACE established an independent inquiry into the future of lifelong learning. Its aim was to: '… offer an authoritative, coherent strategic framework for lifelong learning in the UK' (NIACE, 2009: 5). The resulting report, *Learning Through Life* (Schuller and Watson, 2009), proposed a new policy model for lifelong learning and a 'rebalancing' of funding to reflect a commitment to learning across the life course. Its recommendations form the basis of NIACE's work in attempting to influence government and others of the value of adult education and lifelong learning. To date, there is little evidence of a positive response from government.

National membership organisations: Strengths and limitations

The strength of national membership organisations is in their ability to work both horizontally – in cross-sector alliances, and vertically – as a conduit between their membership and those who make or implement policy. In so doing, they can link 'action and experience at the "micro" (grass roots) and the "macro" (global) level' (Edwards, 1993: 165), creating a productive synergy between the two. National membership organisations enjoy a degree of organisational stability which enables them to undertake sustained advocacy. This may involve research, information gathering and relationship building. Reaping benefits from these activities may take time and resources, which short-run campaigns rarely have at their disposal. Equally, membership organisations run the risk of seeming distant or tokenistic in their approach to their membership, prioritising building relationships with those who have influence rather than with those who work in the field. At the same time, with membership revenues dropping through the loss of grass roots funding, membership organisations themselves can become dependent on government funding and goodwill for their own survival (Leipold, 2000). This potentially compromises an organisation's independence and freedom to advocate. It also implicates the organisation within the neoliberal culture of contracting out of public services (Edwards, 1993).

In the interviews with adult educators in both countries, tensions between the perspectives of practitioners at the grass roots and their membership organisations were apparent. In England, few of the practitioners interviewed made any connections with NIACE as an organisation advocating on their behalf except those who had themselves worked at a national level within or alongside NIACE. In New Zealand, at the time the interviews took place, the divergence in perspectives between grass roots adult educators and ACE Aotearoa appeared particularly marked:

> *It seems like there's a shift in ACE Aotearoa away from Branches... towards collaboration with local authority organisations and government bodies. There seems to be a shift in the type of organisation ACE Aotearoa has become.* (Gina, New Zealand, part-time, adult educator, 25 years)

> *ACE Aotearoa has become the contract holder for Tertiary Education Commission. So they have got confused about their role as upholding the kaupapa of ACE Aotearoa and being the implementer of TEC contracts.* (Ann, New Zealand, full-time unpaid educator, 30 years plus)

Over the preceding five years the focus of ACE Aotearoa had shifted from advocating on behalf of locally-based adult educators to influencing and implementing government policy as a contract holder. In this sense it had become more managerial and less adversarial.

Membership organisations are well placed to collect and collate evidence and opinions from learners and education at grass roots level. However, there is clearly a tension between the representative and advocacy roles of membership organisations and their role as contractors for government. This suggests that attention needs to be paid to the ways in which such organisations consult and communicate with their members. It also suggests their need to be clear about the terms of government support and the implications of accepting it.

Grass roots campaigns

Grass roots campaigns may spring up spontaneously in response to a specific issue or policy change or they may be more deliberatively organised (Chapman and Fisher, 2000). They tend to focus on mobilising learners, educators and the public and on responding to immediate events, through the media, petitions or through organising a physical lobbying presence.

New Zealand: Stop Night Class Cuts!

The 'Stop Night Class Cuts!' campaign was launched in 2009 by CLASS (Community Learning Association through Schools). It stimulated public activity, media coverage and parliamentary discussion around the cuts in ACE funding which were announced shortly after the election of the National Government in 2008. The campaign united adult education providers, teachers and learners in an array of events around the country which highlighted the impact of the cuts (Fordyce and Papa, 2010; Tully, 2010). These included a national day of action which was held during Adult Learners' Week. A petition, signed by over 50,000 people, was delivered to parliament and adult education was, for a while, a topic of parliamentary debate. However, the campaign did not result in the reversal of the cuts or a government change of heart. Programme closures and job losses went ahead. The campaign was lively, but short lived; funding cuts affected its ability to mobilise as schools and community organisations which continued to offer adult education opportunities sought to survive in the changed funding climate. The Stop Night Class Cuts! campaign was spontaneous and imaginative but ultimately it could not survive the loss of its key members to redundancies. Nor was its base sufficiently wide (particularly given the relatively scattered and isolated nature of its practitioners) for it to be able to form a coherent national campaign of opposition.

England: Action for ESOL

Action for ESOL is a broad-based campaign involving ESOL practitioners and learners, national bodies, trade unions, community organisations and public sector employees across the UK. It emerged from a seminar of ESOL practitioners and others held in 2011 in response to the continuing erosion of learners' eligibility for subsidised language classes. The seminar, entitled *'Where have we come from, where are we now? And where are we going?'* stimulated a year of discussion which culminated in the publication of the ESOL Manifesto (Action for ESOL, 2012), a statement of beliefs and values about the importance of well-funded, high-quality language education in a socially just and democratic society. The manifesto also made the case for pay and conditions which reflect the skill and training that ESOL educators bring to their work. The Action for ESOL Campaign continues, through email networking, online bulletins, lobbying and responding to policy pronouncements, such as the government annual spending review (Action for ESOL, 2013).

Practitioner campaigns: strengths and limitations

The energy generated by grass roots campaigns has the capacity to capture public and media attention in ways which years of 'back channel' advocacy, evidence gathering and relationship-building cannot (Chapman and Fisher, 2000; Leipold, 2000). They can mobilise practitioners and learners and create a sense of shared purpose, drawing on the commitment of those involved. They can utilise informal communication channels and thereby react quickly to changing events in innovative ways. They also have the potential to promote informal transformational learning (Foley, 1999). In this respect the Action for ESOL campaign has been particularly successful in mobilising opinion and action – and in winning some concessions. It was widely cited by English adult educators as an example of the power of grass roots campaigns:

> *It's a real bottom up campaign… It's so creative; it's so imaginative and it takes me right back to my first days in adult education… And I think some of the most interesting discussions about adult pedagogy are taking place in ESOL, which is interesting.* (Dennis, England, full-time co-ordinator, 30 years plus)

> *I think with ESOL we have had small concessions because people have got very 'arsey' and said that this is just not civilised… A lot*

of them of them have fought to be here and they come from cultures where you have to fight. We could learn a lot from them. (Sue, England, full-time ESOL teacher, 25 years)

However, the limitations of active opposition are obvious. Adult educator jobs are insecure and the learners whose education is subject to cuts may lack political clout. Furthermore, adult educators lack industrial muscle and have little bargaining power beyond the mobilisation of public opinion. There are also dilemmas for individual adult educators involving themselves in campaigning – whether they risk their already precarious positions or whether, having lost their employment, they can realistically carry on campaigning. Ongoing cuts to funding and the contraction of the adult education workforce therefore starve campaigns of key activists and make them susceptible to collapse:

The people [the cuts in services] affect are the people who are the least able to make a noise about it really. And historically it's been the educators themselves who would make a noise about it. And that's quite a responsibility in a way. We're not allowed to, because we work for the Council, we're not allowed to campaign. But the people using community education are the least powerful. (Ursula, England, full-time community learning manager, 26 years)

… if I decide to do lobbying or campaigning or something, I still have to have an ordinary everyday role which is who I am and where I stand… You can't just be a political activist, just like that… We still have to do what we do; what is us, even if we decide that the most important thing is the political action… (Imogen, New Zealand, part-time adult educator and volunteer, 30 years plus)

Table 8.1 summarises the strengths and limitations of the different forms of advocacy in adult education discussed above. It is likely that at different points in the life of an advocacy or campaigning organisation it will adopt different approaches – persuasive or adversarial, through the media or through research and information gathering. As the literature of international advocacy and campaigning suggests, no one approach is superior to another. Rather, they have the potential to complement and enhance one another (Edwards, 1993; Anderson, 2000; Chapman and Fisher, 2000). However, Edwards (1993: 168) suggests, and the evidence

Table 8.1 Advocacy and campaigning strategies: strengths and limitations

Strategy type	Strengths	Limitations
Strategic alliances	• access to organisational resources • mobilise shared interests • high-level advocacy • access to channels of influence	• remoteness from grass roots concerns • competing agendas • over-identification with target of advocacy
National organisations	• organisational base • organisational profile • continuity • ability to work vertically and horizontally	• remoteness from grass roots concerns • dependence on government goodwill/funding
Grass roots campaigns	• grass roots credibility • potential for learning • informal communication channels • high commitment • ability to respond quickly • innovation and creativity • draw on a range of knowledge and expertise	• narrow focus • resource poor • dependence on key individuals • limited bargaining power • campaigner vulnerability

confirms, that advocacy approaches are subject to four weaknesses: lack of a clear strategy, weakness in alliances, an absence of credible alternatives and the problems inherent in relationships with donor agencies. In relation to adult education, the marginality of the sector and the insecurity of tenure of many of its advocates make its defence a daunting challenge.

Summary: Learning the lessons

I think many organisations have lost that capacity to be embarrassing and to stand up in public and name names and point fingers – in the media and in the press and in public – and be noisy about it... (Carla, England, part-time adult educator and volunteer, 30 years plus)

It is tempting, given the strength and length of the onslaught on adult education to conclude that there is nothing to be done and that the best course of action for the adult educator – as long as she or he is still in employment – is to wait for the policy tide to turn. However, the evidence suggests that while governments may promote particular short-term projects which may not last beyond their tenure in power, policy is not cyclical; 'what goes around' does not 'come around'. Rather, the overall thrust of neoliberalisation has been constant, regardless of the government in power. Policy fatalism as a strategy for survival diminishes individual adult educators' sense of agency and vitiates adult education as an area of practice informed by values of equality and social justice. Furthermore, the idea that adopting approaches that chime in with current government policies (be they called active citizenship, Big Society or social enterprise) will ensure the future for broadly based, accessible and socially just forms of adult education requires critical examination. The evidence suggests that social enterprise as a comprehensive approach to public sector provision is likely to be neither feasible nor equitable.

More active, collaborative responses are required if any impression is to be made on the direction of travel of current policy. Advocacy and campaigning strategies represent attempts to influence the agenda and, perhaps, to change policy. However, the relative lack of bargaining power of adult educators as workers and the marginality of adult education as a sector mean that they are likely to make little impact by themselves. Regional, national – or even international – advocacy and campaigning for adult education cannot divert an ideological tide which extends much further than adult education and which is backed by the resources of powerful governments working in concert. However, they can make a valuable contribution towards doing so (Edwards, 1993). They can raise awareness and shine a crucial light on injustices and inconsistencies in policy. They can also activate people, and they have the potential for transformational learning. The following chapter draws some of the conclusions from the research on which this book is based and some of the ways in which an agenda for a socially just and transformative adult education might be taken forward.

CONCLUSION

Lessons for changing times

*Adult education is an exceptionally diverse field whose practitioners
do not all share a common professional culture, or even a common
term to designate what it is they do. Debates among adult educators
are accordingly informed – or ill-informed – by an inadequate
theoretical base and distorted by terminological and conceptual
confusions. Where these debates are concerned with vital political
questions of direction, purpose, the exercise of power and the
allocation of resources, theoretical weakness can have serious practical
consequences, making it hard for practitioners to understand the
situations in which they find themselves and unsure what action to
take. Where politics is concerned, while knowledge may not always be
power, ignorance is rarely bliss.* (Coben, 1998: 5)

*We can capitulate and become more efficient managers of learning
for capitalism. We can nostalgically and ineffectually bemoan the
decline and death of earlier traditions. Or we can fight on new terrain.*
(Foley, 2001: 84)

Introduction

This book set out to explore the impact of globally circulating ideology
and discourse on adult educators and their work. It focused on England
and New Zealand, two countries which, though geographically distant from each other, share political, economic, social and cultural
commonalities whose origins lie in British colonial expansion in the
eighteenth and nineteenth centuries. More recently, they have shared

the experience of the application of neoliberalising policies in the public sector, including adult education. In England and New Zealand, as elsewhere, the development of organised forms of adult education has been accompanied by contestation over its aims, content and pedagogy. One central question concerning these aims is the extent to which education should be a force for social change operating critically and independently of the prevailing political, social and economic order, or whether efforts should be directed towards securing publicly funded provision for the benefit of the general population. Linked to the question of publicly funded education are two further ones: who should benefit from it – and for what ends should it be organised? These debates are echoed in contemporary struggles over the future of adult education (CCCS, 1981; Mayo and Thompson, 1995; Thompson, 1997; Foley, 1999).

For over three decades from the second half of the twentieth century there was a measure of consensus in the industrialised world that adult education, broadly defined and for a range of individual, social and economic purposes, was the legitimate responsibility of governments. During this period a key concern was to encourage educational participation across all sections of society, but particularly among people who were less likely to engage in education after leaving school – those who were unemployed and on low incomes, women with caring responsibilities, people with language and literacy needs, older people, people living in rural areas and those with the lowest levels of school achievement (McGivney, 1990; Edwards *et al.*, 1993). An approach that encouraged participation across the board enabled a range of adult education activities to be organised in formal and informal contexts and sustained through the paid work of adult educators. They, in turn, were tacitly or explicitly influenced by diverse philosophical positions and traditions – liberal and humanist and radical – which had been articulated through the struggles that surround education's past. Since the late 1970s, however, the consensus around adult education for personal, cultural and social – as well as economic – development has been overshadowed by a different policy consensus stemming from the global spread of neoliberal ideas into the educational sphere (Gordon and Whitty, 1997; Bourdieu, 1998; Apple, 2000, 2001; Giroux, 2003; Harvey, 2005). This has resulted in policy shifts in adult education and training towards:

- an emphasis on instrumentalist and economic ends rather than a broad range of social and individual purposes;
- marketisation of any provision which does not meet tightly defined policy priorities;
- an assumption that participation in education and training is an individual responsibility – and a necessary condition for social inclusion;
- 'targeting' particular groups deemed to be in need of education and training at the expense of subsidised education for all those wishing to participate;
- tighter monitoring and control of the work of adult educators.

These shifts have presented challenges for adult educators who seek to sustain a working life in adult education as funding cutbacks and job losses have heightened their insecurity and uncertainty about the future. In addition, the shifts have changed the nature of adult educators' work, presenting them with dilemmas about how to reconcile social justice values with the narrower, individualised and instrumentalist expectations laid upon them in the new policy order. This final chapter first revisits the findings from research conducted with adult educators in England and New Zealand in the changing ideological and economic landscape. It goes on to suggest some lessons about adult education practice and its links to theory, as well as strategies which might be adopted by those committed to broadly-based, publicly-funded adult education and the alliances they need to build with others to achieve their ends.

Adult educators as professional workers

The historical reality of adult education as a field of work, for women in particular, is that it is dominated by casual, hourly-paid contracts and the expenditure of emotional labour, usually well beyond the employment contract. Full-time, permanent contracts are relatively rare and usually available only to those working in larger educational institutions (such as universities or colleges) or in national organisations. Casual, flexible work arrangements have suited some – as a 'fall-back' career, rather than a main job. However, this state of affairs has tended to work against adult educators' identifying themselves as members of an organised, unionised workforce. Furthermore, adult education's historical association with a radical or socially ameliorating mission has brought with it a strong tradition of voluntarism in the sector. It has been common (particularly, for example, in literacy and language teaching) for some adult educators to give their services without payment. Moreover, even for those employed as hourly-paid adult educators, the line between paid and voluntary work has often been blurred by the tendency to 'go the extra mile' for learners with whom they work. Taken together, these factors have left adult educators, as workers, open to exploitation and poorly organised to defend their pay, their conditions of work and the quality of service they seek to offer. Against the background of a more generalised attack on public sector expenditure and its resultant impact on job security, adult educators have been extremely vulnerable to job losses. Running alongside the deterioration in their working conditions and job prospects in both England and New Zealand have been government exhortations to them to 'raise quality' through engaging in structured processes of accredited training, professional development and ongoing monitoring. These exhortations have been accompanied by promises of improved professional status and/or enhanced sector funding. In both countries, national organisations representing the interests of adult education and its practitioners have been implicated in the imposition of governmental forms of professionalism either through their involvement in the development of professional bodies for adult educators (as in England), or as contractors with government to co-ordinate professional development activities (as in New Zealand). While the concern of these organisations to raise the status and profile of adult education is an entirely legitimate one, the extent to which it has been enacted on managerialist terrain is problematic. In Chapter Three I traced the background to the debates over professionalisation in the adult education. I argued that the notions of 'professionalism' and 'professionalisation' have been co-opted by governments in both countries for the purpose of performance management. Thus conceived, it is far removed from the ideas of autonomous judgement, ethical practice and public service which have been traditionally associated with professional practice.

Attempts have been made by writers such as Goodson (2003) and Sachs (2003) to re-assert 'principled' or 'transformative' forms of professionalism, characterised by engagement with social and moral purpose, an ethic of care and a culture of collaboration. While such propositions are clearly attractive to adult educators and those who represent them, they pay insufficient attention to the realities of adult educators' working lives and the impact of the educational marketplace

156

and performative regimes on their ability to claim space for the kind of activist professionalism which Goodson and Sachs propose. Some of the realities of adult education practice in the current climate are described in Section Two of this book. The portraits of English and New Zealand adult educators suggest that, by and large, they are already ethical, experienced and well-qualified practitioners who have the knowledge, skills and values associated with professionalism, and call into question the policy preoccupation with the professionalisation agenda. It is interesting to note that in the interviews for this research adult educators rarely bemoaned their lack of professional status: their concerns were more often focused on lack of opportunities and resources – for themselves and for learners.

The low status of adult education as a field of work reflects the continuing low status of non-formal, adult-focused education, the gendered nature of adult education work below the level of management and the relative weakness of adult educators' industrial organisation. The concern over professionalism on the part of government – and some of the organisations which advocate for adult education – diverts attention from the central issues: their marginalisation as workers in a sector of education, their relative isolation and their lack of collective power. Confronting these issues requires collective organisation, independent of government funding. Adult educators' interests as paid workers lie with organised labour rather than in membership of 'professionalised' bodies of workers.

Principled practitioners: Adult educators' relationship to theory

In his discussion of what unites adult and community educators in New Zealand, Robert Tobias suggests that, notwithstanding their varied work contexts and their different ways of interpreting their philosophy and purpose, they can still find common ground:

> ... *provided there is broad acceptance that a key goal of adult educators should be to work towards greater equality and social justice and an explicit recognition and acceptance of differences, there is considerable value in adult and community educators of widely different persuasions and backgrounds coming together to engage in dialogue and undertaking strategic political action and advocacy.*
> (1996a: 59–61)

The evidence from the research undertaken for this book is that there was indeed no consensus as to the philosophical underpinnings of practice and no clear distinction between social and individually focused purposes. However, by and large, adult educators' values and beliefs were expressed in a desire to promote equality of access and opportunity, to compensate for past educational disadvantages and (particularly in New Zealand) to foster social and community cohesion. It is therefore not surprising that, although few of them would have been described as radical, most saw a disjunction between their views about the purpose of adult education and the instrumentalist, marketised and target-driven assumptions under which they were expected to work. In this sense adult educators across the spectrum did seem to share some common ground from which they might seek to challenge the dominant policy orthodoxy.

However, there was some reluctance on the part of adult educators to engage with theory or with an analysis of the ideological and political context for adult education practice. A number of reasons can be advanced to account for this. First, it has been suggested that adult educators tend to shy away from critical analysis of the philosophy and politics of adult education because they see themselves as 'practical people' concerned to get the job done, emphasising pragmatism and flexibility, and put off by what they regard as the alien language of theory (Coben, 1998; Ledwith, 2007; Bowl, 2010). This aversion to theoretical discussion may also reflect a more general contemporary disengagement from political debate, in a situation where the belief has become commonplace that there is no alternative to public sector cutbacks (Giroux, 2001, 2003, 2006). Second, the fragmentation of the field militates against dialogue and debate. Many adult educators who remain in employment work in relative isolation and on casual contracts. As such, they have limited opportunities to debate the purpose of their work with others and limited time and money to attend the conferences and meetings at which adult education is discussed in its wider context. For those newer to the field or whose adult education work has been assimilated into more institutional forms of education (for example, in colleges, polytechnics and mainstream university departments), discussion around adult education's purposes are likely to be marginal. However, 'theoretical weakness' may leave practitioners without the means to articulate their purpose, beyond a generalised commitment to an ethic of care (Coben, 1998).

Even where adult educators were willing to cite theoretical influences, their awareness of contemporary adult education theory was limited and sometimes partial. The most prominently cited theoretical influence was Freire. As discussed in Chapter Five, Freire's work was most often interpreted with reference to individual, student-centred or humanistic approaches to teaching. This tendency for Freire's work to be voided of its political meaning is one which has been noted elsewhere (Freire, 1985; Allman, 1988; Coben, 1998). Two issues arise from this. First, what is useful theory in adult education for neoliberal times and second, how can adult educators as 'public intellectuals' (Giroux, 2001, 2003, 2006) work alongside others to advance a conception of adult education oriented to equality and social justice?

'Really useful' theory: Gramsci and Freire

Although not mentioned by the adult educators interviewed for this book, the work of Gramsci (1971), together with that of Freire (1972, 1973), suggest political and pedagogical lessons for adult educators who are struggling to interpret their work in the current climate (Coben, 1998; Mayo, 1999). Gramsci's writings on the workings of hegemony, the distinction between 'common sense' and 'good sense' understandings, and the role of the adult educator provide the basis of a critical understanding of the politics of adult education. Freire's critique of didactic approaches to education and his advocacy of dialogue and consciousness-raising draw attention to adult education as a political practice. Both Freire and Gramsci were concerned with the working of power and the role of education in exposing and changing power relations, making their work relevant to the current context.

The concept of hegemony (Gramsci, 1971) describes the way in which prevailing power relations are maintained through inculcating dominant values, beliefs, norms and discourses, which come to be viewed as 'common sense'. Hegemonic discourses around education in New Zealand and England can be discerned in the acceptance of the market and of retrenchment as a necessary policy for economic well-being, and the economy as the pre-eminent driver of policy. In the field of adult education the need for fiscal stringency and skills training for employability have come to be regarded as common sense (ibid.) and therefore remain largely uncontested, even in the responses of adult education advocacy organisations. Through a critical lens, however, policy decisions to redirect resources away from broadly-based adult education, in the name of 'targeted' funding, may be seen as cover for a neoliberal agenda – which is indeed contestable. Esland (1990), Coffield (1999, 2000), Avis (2007) and others have offered evidence-based arguments which refute the assertions underpinning the narrowing of education to an economic and instrumentalist endeavour. Likewise, the notion that there is no alternative to public sector cutbacks is contestable (Fisher, 2009; PCSU, 2010). Given the pervasive nature of neoliberal ideas, evidence-based counter-arguments are unlikely to be located in policy pronouncements, but are more likely to be found in the publications of the critics of capitalism (Fisher, 2009; Little, 2010; Grayson and Rutherford, 2010). A reading of these texts suggests that, contrary to common-sense belief, there *are* alternatives to slashing public spending and the revitalisation of progressive alliances is vital to achieving a new consensus which is not based solely on economic priorities (Hall and Massey, 2010). Recognition of the operation of ideological hegemony in relation to adult education opens up the possibility of counter-hegemonic action and enables one to argue, not about the size of the funding cake, the slice which goes to adult education, or who should be given the crumbs from the table but about the nature and ownership of the cake itself.

This has pedagogical implications. For Gramsci (1971) and Freire (1972, 1973) the role of adult educators and their allies is to provide the conditions for people to reflect on their experience, placing it in a wider historical, social and political context, and identifying those 'limit situations' (Freire, 1972: 71) that are obstacles to progressive change, but that can be changed through collective action. A consideration of theory provides adult educators with the tools for progressive political and pedagogical practice. Gramsci's description of hegemony and of the difference between 'common sense' and 'good sense' understandings enables the unmasking of neoliberal ideologies and their influence on adult education policy and practice. The struggle to reclaim adult education for social justice is sustained through making visible the contradictions and injustices of current policies.

Freire's importance in adult education is indisputable and it is evident from this research that his influence on the value base of adult educators and on their conceptions of good pedagogy has been profound. His (1972) critique of banking education and his exposition of a dialogic approach resonates with many adult educators. However, in educational environments dominated by expectations concerning the achievement of pre-ordained outcomes judged by means of fixed assessment regimes there are practical obstacles to dialogue, including lack of time and a narrow curricular focus. Nevertheless, spaces remain within adult education for the exercise of agency. Some adult educators are still willing and able to encourage discussion beyond the immediate context of a prescribed curriculum and consciously foster a questioning approach. This was most clearly apparent among adult educators working with learners experiencing marginalisation and discrimination due to their immigration status.

However, the research for this book suggests that the use of language of liberatory education requires critical scrutiny, as it has been implicated in securing compliance to neoliberalism. The most striking example can be seen in the uses to which the term 'empowerment' has been turned. Even in its Freirean sense, the idea that the educator can legitimately empower learners is problematic (Ellsworth, 1989). Claims to empower raise questions about the nature of power in the relationship between educator and learner and the power possessed by the educator. Questions requiring critical scrutiny in any educational context include:

- How is power (and the lack of it) being defined and by whom?
- What are the political and economic circumstances in which power differentials have arisen?
- Who authorises the adult educators' power?
- To what extent does the adult educator possess power and in relation to whom?
- How are the outcomes of attempts to empower inscribed and assigned value?

The language of empowerment is everywhere. It pervades social work, business and even penal policy (see for example Hannah-Moffat, 2000 for a discussion of its use in women's prisons in Canada). It has been co-opted by governments to shift the discourse of public provision from one of rights to one of responsibilities. Wright (2012) describes the 'fantasy of empowerment' as it has been rolled out in UK education policy since the late 1970s. Empowerment, defined from a neoliberal perspective has become imbued with individualised meaning and used as a tool for promoting education as a commodity. Individuals, through this new meaning, are to be empowered only insofar as they have

161

the resources to choose from among the educational offerings in the marketplace. And if – through lack of money or lack of success within the system – they are not able to capitalise on what is available, they are regarded as responsible for their own disempowerment. Failure to gain prescribed qualifications becomes a personal failure to meet the demands of the 'knowledge economy'. Failure to find work, even in the midst of an unemployment crisis, becomes a failure to secure the necessary 'employment' or 'life skills'. The means to empowerment is training for work or the purchase of more qualifications in the educational market. Empowerment has thus come to be construed as a personal responsibility and disempowerment an individual deficit.

Adult educators need to view their own claims to empower self-critically:

> ... *concepts like participation, empowerment, social justice and equality are not just pleasant and friendly ideas but come from a participatory world view – one which is founded on co-operation and true democracy rather than competition and free market politics.* (Ledwith, 2007: 11)

Crucially, adult educators should regard with suspicion all claims to empower – in particular, policy claims to do so. One of the ways in which adult educators can resist the 'common-sense' assumptions of neoliberal hegemony, with little risk to themselves, is to subject the language used in daily practice to some critical scrutiny and to ask: can the discourse of empowerment and student-centredness (the language of radical and humanist adult education) be reconciled with the discourse of 'delivery' of the 'curriculum' and 'learning packages' (the discourse of the market) and what do these discourses imply about how learning and the learner are conceptualised?

Adult educators as agents for change: Tactics and strategies

There is little doubt that the space for adult educators to exercise agency in the current policy climate has become severely constrained. Targeting, outcomes measurement and tighter monitoring have reduced their room for creative and flexible working. Job insecurity has introduced an element of risk into efforts to challenge 'common sense' ideas about the pre-eminence of economic goals and the privatisation of adult education provision. This state of affairs engenders a sense of powerlessness and may lead some adult educators to direct their efforts towards accommodating the new policy order (for example, around the imposition of fees) by finding ways to turn constraints to advantage. However, local strategies of accommodation are unlikely to be successful in the longer term, since they tend to distort the values on which many adult educators premise their work, drawing them into another value system and giving rise to confusion and demoralisation. Moreover, tactics of accommodation are likely to fall foul of relatively minor changes in policy or personnel. The policy changes which adult educators face go well beyond adult education – and well beyond one country. They are not amenable to local resolution.

However, in different ways, some of the adult educators interviewed for this book were engaged in tactical work to hold on to – or even extend – the boundaries of the shrinking terrain of adult education. They were taking advantage of 'agentic moments' to enact micro-resistances to confound or subvert policy prescriptions, again at the local level. 'Dodging and weaving' or 'working outside the box' involved making on-the-ground judgements about how to resist policy in practice. Such resistances require considerable confidence and critical reflection on the part of the resister. Because they demand a lot of the individual they are likely to be easier for adult educators who are experienced and whose work is underpinned by a strong sense of values. While the possibilities and limitations of micro-resistances need to be carefully weighed in the balance, they nevertheless keep open a space for considering approaches to adult education other than those currently dominating the policy scene.

In Chapter Eight I considered some of the strategic organisational responses to the current crises in adult education, their strengths and limitations. In England and New Zealand, cross-sector strategic alliances and focused campaigns have been mounted in an attempt to influence policy. Strategic alliances may vary in the extent to which they involve educators and learners. In England, the CALL campaign had some success in mobilising grass-roots practitioner support. In New Zealand, the strategic alliance for adult and community education was largely confined to 'high-level' policy work and approaches to government departments and politicians. Experience from the international development field suggests that strategic work enacted principally at a policy level is likely to have limited impact unless it is backed up by public and media pressure (Leipold, 2000). Organisations which focus on developing dialogue with government run the risk of incorporation into its agendas if they fail to keep sufficient distance from government concern, particularly if they are themselves dependent on government funding. They also risk alienation from their grass roots if they fail to build their strategies from the ground up, or to ensure that communication channels to the grass roots have the same kind of priority as the development of 'back channels' with government.

The strength of campaigning is that it can 'catch a moment' of public concern and organise rapid and vocal responses which may embarrass, persuade or pressurise for change. Implicit in public campaigning is the potential to link with other issues in the wider political arena, as well as promoting collective 'learning in action' (Foley, 1999). One of the lessons of the 1960s and 1970s is the way that feminist, anti-war and anti-apartheid campaigns built confidence, engendered wider debate and fostered alliances with other campaigns which enlarged the space for further debate and action and the development of radical ideas and approaches. Movements for equality and democracy go hand in hand with educational activity (Allman, 1999, 2001). But public campaigning, without a clear and credible alternative vision which links to wider public concerns, is unlikely to be effective or sustainable. Advocacy and campaigning strategies, coupled with the development of evidentially and theoretically informed argument, all need to be mobilised in the service of movements for change. Below I suggest some of the features of successful advocacy and campaigning, based on the interviews with adult educators and the literature which discusses advocacy and campaigning strategies in the contexts of international development and the broader field of education.

Some features of successful advocacy and campaigning strategies are that they:

- are inclusive of learners, educators, organisations and the wider public
- have clearly articulated aims developed through debate and consultation
- make the links with underlying political and economic causes
- are able to respond quickly and coherently to policy developments

- build awareness of underlying issues and promote 'learning in action'
- link deliberately with other campaigns, both national and international
- utilise research to generate evidence
- maintain independence from government influence
- actively rebut the opposition's arguments
- are highly interactive
- build on the expertise of all involved.

On their own, advocacy and campaigning around adult education will not change the global agenda. However, they can raise awareness, activate people and – most importantly – link with wider debates and campaigns around neoliberal-inspired policies at a global level. Adult educators are workers and citizens; like many of the learners with whom they work, their livelihoods have become increasingly insecure. Perhaps at no time in the last 20 years has it been clearer that the ideology on which neoliberalism rests does not operate in the interests of working-class or unemployed people. Nor does education – whether first or second chance – any longer guarantee employment or a prosperous future. Their campaigns to protect education as a right for all cannot be divorced from the campaigns of others, and their resistance cannot be maintained successfully in the context of the classroom, the institution or the sector alone (Giroux, 2003; Hatcher, 2007).

Summary: Where is the 'new terrain' in the struggle for adult education?

One of the conclusions of this book is that the space for practitioner agency is, in reality, limited. But that is not to underplay the importance of adult educators in their daily practice, challenging the ways in which both the policy and the language around adult education and training operate against equality and social justice. There is a place for research which evaluates and documents educators' tactics of resistance and highlights what can be learned from their engagements with the day-to-day dilemmas of practice in neoliberal times (Foley, 2001). Similarly, the potential for advocacy and campaigning around adult education is yet to be fully exploited and there are lessons to be learned from these ongoing efforts, some of which have been suggested in this chapter. Therefore a further role for research, in support of advocacy and campaigning work, is to continue to investigate the evidence base for neoliberal claims about the links between training for employment and the development of a 'knowledge economy', and to monitor the social impact of the withdrawal of public funding from adult education.

While the impact of neoliberal ideas on adult education in England and New Zealand may differ in the detail, the outcomes for adult educators as workers have been remarkably similar. Not only these two countries, but also Australia and parts of Europe and North America, have been affected by the commodification of education. The tendency towards parochialism in adult education practice remains strong, in spite of the accessibility of information about international developments assisted by the spread of new technologies. Academics and those working at senior levels in national adult education organisations have ready access to intelligence about the international dimensions of adult education. One little-mentioned professional development need of adult educators, which can be met by their representative bodies and by adult educator trainers, is the cultivation of an international perspective.

However, the fate of adult education is inextricably bound up with the global economic and political order. Responses to attacks upon it therefore also need to be global and political. The reluctance of adult educators to engage in theory and politics is fatal: the need to engage in debate about the purposes of education is more pressing than ever. Yet I would argue that this debate can only successfully be conducted outside the spaces in which adult educators practice as paid workers, and it needs to be conducted independently of government. Moreover, the struggle for education as a public and not a market good can only realistically be successful if it is undertaken in partnership with others who are engaged in arguing for the public provision of education alongside adequate health care and social welfare. Maintaining traditions of critical and radical adult education outside the state is equally important. In this respect the re-birth of radical education and 'people's universities' in the wake of the Occupy protests which took place across the world from 2011 are encouraging (Neary and Amsler, 2012). Educators, along with public sector, anti-poverty and anti-racist campaigners, environmentalists and trades unionists need to link together to determine what kind of education, what kind of state – and what kind of world – we want.

References

Abu-Saifan, S. (2012) 'Social entrepreneurship: definition and boundaries', *Technology Innovation Management Review,* February 2012: 22–27.

ACE Aotearoa (2012) *Annual Report 2012* www.aceaotearoa.org.nz/sites/aceaotearoa.org.nz/files/ACE-AnnualReport-2012-web.pdf (accessed 1 July 2013).

ACE Sector Strategic Alliance (2011) *Real Value: investing in ordinary people: Adult and community education in New Zealand: The next 10 years* Wellington: ACE Sector Strategic Alliance.

Action for ESOL (2012) *The ESOL Manifesto* www.actionforesol.org (accessed 1 June 2013).

Action for ESOL (2013) *Statement on George Osborne's Spending Review of 26 June 2013* www.actionforesol.org (accessed 25 July 2013).

Alexander, R., Osborn, M. and Phillips, D. (2000) *Learning from Comparing,* Wallingford: Symposium Books.

Allaway, A. J. (1961) *The Educational Centres Movement: A comprehensive survey,* London: National Institute of Adult Education.

Allman, P. (1988) 'Gramsci, Freire and Illich' in T. Lovett (ed.) *Radical Approaches to Adult Education: A reader,* London: Routledge.

Allman, P. (1999) *Revolutionary social transformation: Democratic hopes, political possibilities and critical education,* Westport, PA: Bergin and Garvey.

Allman, P. (2001) *Critical education against global capitalism,* Westport, PA: Bergin and Garvey.

Anderson, I. (2000) 'Northern NGO advocacy: Perceptions, reality and the challenge', *Development in Practice* 10 (3 and 4) pp. 445–452, Taylor & Francis.

Apple, M. (2000) 'Can critical pedagogy interrupt rightist policies?' *Educational Theory* 50 (2) pp. 229–254, Wiley.

167

Apple, M. (2001) 'Comparing neo-liberal projects and inequality in education', *Comparative Education* 37 (4) pp. 409–423, Taylor & Francis.

Apps J. W. (1973) *Towards a Working Philosophy of Adult Education,* Syracuse, NY: Syracuse University Publications in Continuing Education.

Armstrong, P. and Miller, N. (2006) 'Whatever happened to social purpose? Adult educators' stories of political commitment and change', *International Journal of Lifelong Education* 25 (3) pp. 291–305, Taylor & Francis.

Avis, J. (1999) 'Shifting identity: new conditions and the transformation of practice – teaching within post-compulsory education', *Journal of Vocational Education & Training* 51 (2) pp. 245–264, Taylor & Francis.

Avis, J. (2005) 'Beyond performativity: reflections on activist professionalism and the labour process in further education', *Journal of Education Policy* 20 (2) pp. 209–222, Taylor & Francis.

Avis, J. (2007) *Education, Policy and Social Justice*, London: Continuum.

Ball, M. J. (2009) 'Learning, labour and employability', *Studies in the Education of Adults* 41 (1) pp. 39–52, Leicester: NIACE.

Ball, S. (2000) 'Performativities and fabrications in the education economy: towards the performative society', *Australian Educational Researcher* 17 (3) pp. 1–24, Springer.

Ball, S. (2003) 'The teacher's soul and the terrors of performativity', *Journal of Education Policy* 18 (2) pp. 215–228, Taylor & Francis.

Ball, S. (2008a) 'Performativity, privatisation, professionals and the State' in B. Cunningham (ed.) *Exploring Professionalism* London: Institute of Education.

Ball, S. (2008b) *The Education Debate*, Bristol: Policy Press.

Ball, S. (2012) 'Performativity, Commodification and Commitment: An I-Spy Guide to the Neoliberal University', *British Journal of Educational Studies* 60 (1) pp. 17–28, Taylor & Francis.

Ball, S. and Goodson, I. (eds.) (1985) *Teachers' Lives and Careers,* Lewes: The Falmer Press.

Bathmaker, A. and Avis, J. (2012) 'Inbound, outbound or peripheral: The impact of discourses of 'organisational' professionalism on becoming a teacher in English further education', *Discourse: Studies in the Cultural Politics of Education* pp. 1–18, Taylor & Francis.

Bathmaker, A. and Harnett, H. (2010) *Exploring Learning, Identity and Power through Life History and Narrative Research,* London: Routledge.

Beck, J. (2008) 'Governmental professionalism: Re-professionalising or de-professionalising teachers in England?' *British Journal of Educational Studies* 56 (20) pp. 119–143, Taylor & Francis.

Beck, J. (2009) 'Appropriating professionalism: restructuring official knowledge base of England's 'modernised' teaching profession', *British Journal of Sociology of Education* 30 (1) pp. 3–14, Taylor & Francis.

Becker, G. S. (1975) *Human Capital: A Theoretical and Empirical Analysis with*

Special Reference to Education, New York: Columbia University Press.

Benn, R. and Burton, R. (1995) 'Access and targeting: an exploration of a contradiction', *International Journal of Lifelong Education* 14 (6) pp. 444–458, Taylor & Francis.

Benseman, J. (2005) 'Paradigm lost: lifelong education in New Zealand in the 1970s and 1980s', *New Zealand Journal of Adult Learning* 33 pp. 6–20, Auckland: University of New Zealand.

Beyer, A. (1981) *Being there: An account of some learning outcomes of participation by a large number of people in direct action in opposition to the 1981 Springbok Tour of New Zealand.* Paper presented at the NZARE Symposium on Education for Change, Hamilton, New Zealand.

Biesta, G. and Tedder, M. (2007) 'Agency and learning in the lifecourse: Towards an ecological perspective', *Studies in the Education of Adults* 39 (2) pp. 132–149, Leicester: NIACE.

BIS (Department for Business, Innovation & Skills) (2009) *Skills for Growth,* London: BIS.

BIS (Department for Business, Innovation & Skills) (2012a) *Professionalism in further education: interim report of the independent review panel,* London: BIS.

BIS (Department for Business, Innovation & Skills) (2012b) *Professionalism in Further Education: Final report of the independent review panel,* London: BIS.

BIS (Department for Business, Innovation & Skills) (2012c) Consultation *on revocation of the further education workforce regulations,* London: BIS.

BIS (Department for Business, Innovation & Skills) (2012d) *Evaluation of FE Teachers' Qualifications (England) Regulations 2007,* London: BIS.

BIS (Department for Business, Innovation & Skills) (2012e) *Community Learning Trusts Pilots: Prospectus,* London: BIS.

Blair, T. (1998) *New Politics for a New Century,* London: Fabian Society.

Boud, D. and Rooney, D. (2010) 'The role of adult educators: more than the grin on the Cheshire Cat?' *Paper presented at the 40th Annual SCUTREA Conference 6–8 July,* University of Warwick, Coventry.

Bourdieu, P. (1998) *Acts of Resistance: Against the New Myths of Our Time,* Cambridge: Polity Press.

Bourzaga, C. and Defourny, J. (2001) *The Emergence of Social Enterprise,* London: Routledge.

Bowl, M. (2007) *Adult and Community Development (ACE) Networks and Professional Development Report to the Tertiary Education Commission,* Christchurch: University of Canterbury.

Bowl, M. (2010) 'University Continuing Education in a Neoliberal Landscape: Developments in England and Aotearoa New Zealand', *International Journal of Lifelong Education* 29 (6) pp. 723–738, Taylor & Francis.

Bowl, M. (2011) 'Communities of practice, compliance or resistance? Regional networks in the Adult and Community Education sector in Aotearoa New

Zealand', *Community Development Journal* 46 (2) pp. 83–91, Oxford: Oxford University Press.

Bowl, M. and Tobias, R. (2012) 'Learning from the past, organising for the future: Adult and Community Education in Aotearoa New Zealand', *Adult Education Quarterly* 62 (3) pp. 272–286, Sage.

Brookfield, S. (1986) *Understanding and Facilitating Adult Learning: A comprehensive analysis of principles and effective practice,* Milton Keynes: Open University Press.

Brookfield, S. (2005) *The Power of Critical Theory for Adult Teaching and Learning,* Maidenhead: Open University Press.

Bruner, J. (1960) *The Process of Education,* Cambridge, Mass: Harvard University Press.

Callaghan, J. (1976) *Ruskin College Oxford Speech* 18th October 1976. www. educationengland.org.uk/documents/speeches/1976ruskin.html (accessed 1 June 2013).

CCCS (Centre for Contemporary Cultural Studies) (1981) *Unpopular Education: schooling and social democracy in England since 1944,* London: Hutchinson.

CEC (Commission of the European Committee) (2007) *Action Plan on Adult Learning – it's always a good time to learn,* Brussels: CEC.

Chapman, J. and Fisher, T. (2000) 'The effectiveness of NGO campaigning: lessons from practice', *Development in Practice* 10 (2) pp. 151–165, Taylor & Francis.

Coare, P. and Johnson, R. (2003) *Adult Learning, Citizenship and Community Voices,* Leicester: NIACE.

Coben, D. (1998) *Radical heroes: Gramsci, Freire and the politics of adult education,* New York: Garland.

Codd, J. (1999) 'Educational reform, accountability and the culture of distrust', *New Zealand Journal of Educational Studies* 34 (1) pp. 45–53.

Codd J. (2002) 'The third way for tertiary education policy: TEAC and beyond', *New Zealand Annual Review of Education* 11 pp. 31–57.

Codd, J. (2005) 'Teachers as "Managed Professionals" in the global education industry: the New Zealand experience', *Educational Review* 57 (2) pp. 193–206, Taylor & Francis.

Coffield, F. (1999) 'Breaking the Consensus: lifelong learning as social control', *British Educational Research Journal* 25 (4) pp. 479–499, Taylor & Francis.

Coffield, F. (ed.) (2000) *Differing Visions of A Learning Society Volume 1,* Bristol: Policy Press.

Corbett, S. and Walker, A. (2012) 'The Big Society: back to the future', *The Political Quarterly,* 83 (3) pp. 487–493, Wiley.

Cranton, P. (1994) *Understanding and Promoting Transformative Learning: A guide for educators of adults,* San Francisco: Jossey Bass.

Crowther, J. (2004) '"In and against' lifelong learning: flexibility and the corrosion of character', *International Journal of Lifelong Education* 23 (2) pp. 125–136, Taylor & Francis.

Dave, R. H. (ed.) (1976) *Foundations of Lifelong Education,* Oxford: Pergamon and UNESCO Institute for Education.

Day, C. (1999) *Developing Teachers: the challenges of lifelong learning,* London: Falmer Press.

Delors, J. (1996) *Learning: the treasure within,* Paris: UNESCO.

Department for Internal Affairs: Te Tari Taiwhenua (2013) *Mapping Social Enterprises in New Zealand: Results of a 2012 survey,* Wellington: Department for Internal Affairs.

DES (Department for Education and Science) (1973) *Adult Education: A plan for development,* London: HMSO.

De Ruyter, A., Kirkpatrick, I., Hoque, K., Lonsdale, C. and Malan, J. (2008) 'Agency working and the degradation of public service employment: the case of nurses and social workers', *The International Journal of Human Resource Management* 19 (3) pp. 432–445, Taylor & Francis.

Dewey, J. (1938) *Education and Experience,* New York: Collier Books.

DfEE (Department for Education and Employment) (1998) *The Learning Age: A renaissance for a new Britain,* London: HMSO.

DfES (Department for Education and Skills) (2001) *The Post-16 Education and Training Inspection Regulations,* Statutory Instrument 2001 No 799, London: DfES.

DfES (Department for Education and Skills) (2004) *Equipping our Teachers for the Future: reforming initial teacher training for the learning and skills sector,* London: DfES.

DfES (Department for Education and Skills) (2006) *Further Education: Raising Skills, Improving Life Chances,* Norwich: The Stationery Office.

Dore, R. (1997) *The Diploma Disease,* London: Institute of Education.

Ecclestone, K. (2007) 'Editorial – An identity crisis? Using concepts of 'identity', 'agency' and 'structure' in the education of adults', *Studies in the Education of Adults* 39 (2) pp. 121–131, Leicester: NIACE.

Edwards, M. (1993) "Does the doormat influence the boot?': critical thoughts on UK NGOs and international advocacy', *Development in Practice* 3 (3) pp. 163–175, Taylor & Francis.

Edwards, R., Simiensky, S. and Zeldin, D. (1993) *Adult Learners, Education and Training,* Leicester: NIACE.

Elias, L. and Merriam, S. B. (1994) *Philosophical Foundations of Adult Education,* Malabar: Kreiger.

Ellsworth, E. (1989) "Why doesn't this feel empowering?' Working through the repressive myths of critical pedagogy', *Harvard Educational Review* 59 (3) pp. 297–324, Harvard Education Publishing Group.

Emirbayer, M. and Mische, A. (1998) 'What is agency?' *American Journal of Sociology* 103(4) pp. 962–1023, Chicago: University of Chicago Press.

Epstein, A. (1978) *Ethos and Identity,* London: Tavistock.

Eraut, M. (1994) *Developing Professional Knowledge and Competence,* London: Falmer.

Esland, G. (1990) *Education, Training and Employment Vol. 2: The educational response,* Wokingham: Addison-Wesley.

Etzioni, A. (1969) *The Semi-professions and their organisation: Teachers, nurses and social workers,* New York: The Free Press.

Faure, E. (1972) *Learning to Be: the world of education today and tomorrow,* Paris: UNESCO.

Feldman, D. (2006) 'Towards a new taxonomy for understanding the nature of and consequences of contingent employment', *Career Development International* 11(1) pp. 28–47, Emerald.

FENTO (Further Education National Training Organisation) (1999) *Standards for Teaching and Supporting Learning in Further Education in England and Wales,* London: FENTO.

Fenwick, T. (2010) 'Accountability practices in adult education: insights from actor-network theory', *Studies in the Education of Adults* 42 (2) pp. 170–185, Leicester: NIACE.

Field, J. (2000) *Lifelong Learning and the New Educational Order,* Stoke-on-Trent: Trentham.

Fieldhouse, R. (1996) *A History of Modern British Adult Education,* Leicester: NIACE.

Fisher, M. (2009) *Capitalist realism: Is there no alternative?* Winchester: Zero Books.

Fitzgerald, T. (2008) 'The continuing politics of mistrust: performance management and the erosion of professional work', *Journal of Educational Administration and History* 40 (2) pp. 113–128, Taylor & Francis.

Flexner, P. (1915) 'Is social work a profession?' *School and Society* 1 pp. 901–911, Chicago: University of Chicago Press.

Foley, G. (1999) *Learning in Social Action,* Leicester: NIACE.

Foley, G. (2001) 'Radical adult education and learning', *International Journal of Lifelong Education* 2 (1–2) pp. 71–88, Taylor & Francis.

Fordyce, M. and Papa, M. (2009) 'Government Cuts to Adult and Community Education: A CLASS response', *Journal of Adult Learning Aotearoa New Zealand* 37(2) pp. 6–9.

Freire, P. (1972) *Pedagogy of the Oppressed,* Harmondsworth: Penguin.

Freire, P. (1973) *Cultural Action for Freedom,* New York: Seabury.

Freire, P. (1985) *The Politics of Education: culture, power and liberation,* Westport: Bergin and Garvey.

Fryer, R. H. (2010) *Promises of Freedom: Chitzenship, belonging and lifelong learning,* Leicester: NIACE.

Gewirtz, S. and Ball, S. (2000) 'From 'Welfarism' to 'New Managerialism': shifting discourses of school leadership in the education market place', *Discourse* 21 (3) pp. 253–267.

Ghaye, A. and Ghaye, K. (1998) *Teaching and Learning through Critical Reflective Practice*, London: David Fulton.

Giddens, A. (1990) *The Consequences of Modernity*, Cambridge: Polity Press.

Giddens, A. (1998) *The Third Way: The Renewal of Social Democracy*, Cambridge: Polity Press.

Giddens, A. (2000) *The Third Way and its Critics*, Cambridge: Polity Press.

Giddens, A. (ed.) (2001) *The Global Third Way Debate*, Cambridge: Polity Press.

Giroux, H.A. (2001) *Public Spaces and Private Lives: beyond the culture of cynicism*, Lanham: Rowman and Littlefield.

Giroux, H. A. (2003) 'Public pedagogy and the politics of resistance: notes on a critical theory of educational struggle', *Educational philosophy and theory* 35 (1) pp. 5–16, Wiley.

Giroux, H. A. (2006) *America on the Edge: Henry Giroux on politics, culture and education*, Gordonsville: Palgrave Macmillan.

Goodson, I. (1994) 'Studying the teacher's life and work', *Teaching and Teacher Education* 10 (1) pp. 29–37, Elsevier.

Goodson, I. (2003) *Professional Knowledge, Professional Lives*, Maidenhead: Open University Press.

Goodson, I. F. and Hargreaves, A. (eds.) (1996) *Teachers' Professional Lives*, London: Falmer Press.

Gordon, L. and Whitty, G. (1997) 'Giving the 'Hidden Hand' a helping hand? The rhetoric and reality of neoliberal education reform in England and New Zealand', *Comparative Education* 33 (3): 453–467, Taylor & Francis.

Gordon, P., Perkin, H., Sockett, H. and Hoyle, E. (1985) *Is Teaching a Profession?* London: Bedford Way Papers.

Govers, E. (2010) 'On the impact of government policy on programme design in New Zealand post-compulsory education' *Research in Post-Compulsory Education* 15 (2) pp. 141–158.

Gramsci, A. (1971) *Selections from the Prison Notebooks of Antonio Gramsci*, edited by Q. Hoare and G. N. Smith, London: ElecBook.

Grant, S. (2008) 'Contextualising social enterprise in New Zealand', *Social Enterprise Journal* 4 (1) pp. 9–23, Emerald.

Grayson, R. S. and Rutherford, J. (2010) *After the crash: Reinventing the left in Britain*, London: Soundings, Social Liberal Forum and Compass.

Groves, B. (2012) 'The trouble with professionals', *Adults Learning* Summer 2012, pp. 40–41, Leicester: NIACE.

Guimarães, P. (2009) 'Reflections on the professionalisation of adult educators in the framework of public policies in Portugal', *European Journal of Education* 44 (2) pp. 205–219, Wiley.

Hake, B. J. (2010) 'Rewriting the history of adult education: the search for narrative structures' *International Encyclopedia of Adult Education and Training (Third edition)*, Oxford: Elsevier.

Hall, D. and Hall, I. (1996) *Practical Social Research,* Basingstoke: Macmillan.

Hall, S. and Massey, D. (2010) 'Interpreting the Crisis', in R. S. Grayson and J. Rutherford (eds.) *After the crash: Reinventing the left in Britain* (pp. 37–46), London: Soundings, Social Liberal Forum and Compass.

Handy, C. (1994) *The Empty Raincoat,* London: Random House.

Hannah-Moffat, K. (2000) 'Prisons that Empower: neoliberal governance in Canadian prisons', *British Journal of Criminology* 40 (3) pp. 510–531, Oxford Journals.

Hanson, A. (1996) 'The search for separate theories of adult learning: does anyone really need andragogy?' in R. Edwards, A. Hanson and P. Raggatt (eds.) *Boundaries of Adult Learning: adult learners, education and training Vol. 1,* London: Routledge.

Harber, C. (2009) *Toxic Schooling: How schools became worse,* Nottingham: Heretics Press.

Harrison, T. (1994) *Learning and Living 1790–1960: a study in the history of the English adult education movement,* Aldershot: Gregg Revivals.

Harvey, D. (2005) *A Brief History of Neoliberalism,* Oxford: Oxford University Press.

Hatcher, R. (2007) 'Yes, but how do we get there?' Alternative visions and the problem of strategy', *Journal of Critical Education Policy Studies* 5(2) www.jceps.com/index.php?pageID=article&articleID=98 (accessed 1 October 2010).

Healy, N. and Gunby, P. (2012) 'The Impact of recent government tertiary education policies on access to higher education in New Zealand', *Journal of Educational Leadership, Policy and Practice* 27 (1) pp. 29–45.

Heimstra, R. (1988) 'Translating personal values and philosophy into political action' in R.G. Brockett (ed.) *Ethical Issues in Adult Education,* New York: Columbia University Teachers' College.

Hill, R. S. (2004) *State Authority, Indigenous Autonomy: Crown/Maori Relations in New Zealand/Aotearoa 1900–1950,* Wellington: Victoria University Press.

H.M. Government (2011) *Growing the Social Investment Market: a vision and strategy,* London: The Cabinet Office.

Hodkinson, P. and Sparkes, A. C. (1997) 'Careership: A sociological theory of career decision making', *British Journal of Sociology of Education* 18 (1) pp. 29–44, Taylor & Francis.

Houle (1981) *Continuing Learning in the Professions,* San Francisco: Jossey Bass.

Hoyle, E. (1985) 'The professionalisation of teachers: a paradox' in P. Gordon, H. Perkin, H. Sockett and E. Hoyle *Is Teaching a Profession?* London: Bedford Way Papers.

Huberman, M. (1995) 'Professional careers and professional development and some intersections' in T. Guskey and M. Huberman (eds.) *Professional Development in Education: new perspectives and practices,* New York: Teachers College Press.

174

Hudson, J. W. (1851) *The History of Adult Education,* London: Longman, Brown, Green and Longmans.

Hunt, S. (2011) 'We've broken free of the IfL – but what now?' *FE Focus,* 5 August 2011 www.tes.co.uk/articles.aspx?storycode=6007494 (accessed 11 August 2011).

Hyland, T. (1994) *Competence, Education and NVQs: Dissenting perspectives,* London: Cassell Education.

IfL (Institute for Learning) (2009) *IfL Review of CPD: making a difference for teachers, trainers and learners,* London: IfL.

Illich, I. (1973) *Deschooling Society,* Harmondsworth: Penguin.

Irwin, J. (2012) *Paulo Freire's Philosophy of Education,* London: Continuum.

Irwin, K. (2008) *ACE professional development Hui and Fono evaluation report,* Auckland: Hope Brokers.

Jarvis, P. (ed.) (1987) *Twentieth Century Thinkers in Adult Education,* London: Croom Helm.

Jarvis, P. (ed.) (2011) *The Routledge International Handbook of Lifelong Learning,* Abingdon: Routledge.

Jephcote, M. and Salisbury, J. (2009) 'Further Education Teachers' Accounts of their professional identities', *Teaching and Teacher Education* 25 pp. 966–972, Elsevier.

Johnson, R. (1979) "Really useful knowledge': radical education and working-class culture, 1790–1848' in J. Clarke, C. Critcher and R. Johnson (eds.) *Working Class Culture: studies in history and theory,* London: Hutchinson.

Kelly, T. (1970) A *History of Adult Education in Great Britain,* Liverpool: Liverpool University Press.

Kerlin, J. A. (2009) *Social Enterprise: A Global Comparison,* Medford MA: Tufts University Press.

Kidd, J. M. (1984) 'Young people's perceptions of their occupational decision-making', *British Journal of Guidance and Counselling* 12 pp. 25–38, Taylor & Francis.

King, M. (2003) *The Penguin History of New Zealand,* Auckland: Penguin.

Kirk, J. and Wall, C. (2011) *Work and Identity: historical and cultural contexts,* London: Palgrave Macmillan.

Knowles, M. (1962) *The Adult Education Movement in the United States,* New York: Holt Rinehart & Winston.

Knowles, M. (1973) *The Adult Learner: a neglected species,* Houston: Gulf Publishing.

Krashen, S. D. (1982) *Principles and Practice in Second Language Acquisition,* Oxford: Pergamon.

Krumboltz, J. D. (1979) 'A social learning theory of career decision-making' in A. M. Mitchell, G. B. Jones and J. B. Krumboltz (eds.) *Social Learning and Career Decision Making,* Cranston: Carroll Press.

Larson, M. S. (1979) *The Rise of Professionalism: A sociological analysis,* Berkley: University of California Press.

Lasky, S. (2005) 'A sociocultural approach to understanding teacher identity, agency and professional vulnerability in a context of secondary school reform', *Teaching and Teacher Education* 21 (8) pp. 899–916, Elsevier.

Lawn, M. and Grace, G. (1987) *Teachers: The culture and politics of work,* Lewes: The Falmer Press.

Lawy, R. and Tedder, M. (2009) 'Meeting standards: teacher education in the further education sector: what of the agency of teacher educators?' *Studies in the Education of Adults* 41 (1) pp. 53–67, Leicester: NIACE.

Ledwith, M. (2007) 'Reclaiming the radical agenda: a critical approach to community development', *Concept* 17 (2) pp. 8–12 www.infed.org/community/critical_community_development.htm (accessed 11 April 2013).

Leipold, G. (2000) 'Campaigning: a fashion or the best way to change the global agenda?' *Development in Practice* 10 (3–4) pp. 453–460, Taylor & Francis.

Leitch, S. (2006) *Prosperity for All in the Global Economy: World Class Skills,* London: HMSO.

Lengrand, P. (1970) An *Introduction to Lifelong Education,* Paris: UNESCO.

Lindeman, E. (1926) *The Meaning of Adult Education,* New York: New York Republic.

Little, B. (ed.) (2010) *Radical future: Politics for the next generation,* Middlesex: Soundings/Compass Youth.

Locke, E. (1992) *Peace People: A history of peace activities in New Zealand,* Christchurch: Hazard Press.

Lovett, T. (ed.) (1988) *Radical Approaches to Adult Education: a reader,* London: Routledge.

LSC (Learning and Skills Council) (2000) *Learning and Skills Act 2000* www.legislation.gov.uk/ukpga/2000/21/contents (accessed 30 July 2013).

Lucas, N. and Nasta, T. (2010) 'State regulation and the professionalisation of further education teachers: a comparison with schools and HE', *Journal of Vocational Education and Training* 62(2) pp. 441–454, Taylor & Francis.

Lucas, N., Nasta, T. and Rogers, L. (2012) 'From fragmentation to chaos? The regulation of initial teacher training in further education', *British Educational Research Journal* 38 (4) pp. 677–695, Taylor & Francis.

Luttrell, W. (ed.) (2010) *Qualitative Educational Research,* London: Routledge.

Marriott, S. (1991) 'The journalism of the university extension movement in its political context 1889–1926', *History of Education* 20 (4) pp. 341–357, Taylor & Francis.

Marriott, S. (1998) 'From university extension to extramural studies: conflict and adjustment in English adult education 1911–1939', *Journal of Educational Administration and History* 30 (1) pp. 17–34, Taylor & Francis.

Martin, I. (2001) 'Reconstituting the Agora: Towards an alternative politics of lifelong learning, *Concept* 2 (1) pp. 40–8.

Martin, I. (2005) 'Adult education, lifelong learning and citizenship: some ifs and buts', *International Journal of Lifelong Education* 22 (6) pp. 566–579, Taylor & Francis.

Martin, I. (2006) 'Where have all the flowers gone?' *Adults Learning* October 2006 pp. 15–18, Leicester: NIACE.

Martin, I. (2008) 'Whither adult education in the learning paradigm?' *Keynote Presentation to SCUTREA 2008 38th Annual Conference, Edinburgh, 2–4 July 2008.*

Martin, J. (2010) *Making Socialists: Mary Bridges Adams and the fight for knowledge and power, 1855–1939,* Manchester: Manchester University Press.

Mayo, M. and Thompson, J. (1995) *Adult Learning, Critical Intelligence and Social Change,* Leicester: NIACE.

Mayo, P. (1999) *Gramsci, Freire and Adult Education,* London: Zed Books.

McCulloch, G. (2011) *The Struggle for the History of Education,* Abingdon: Routledge.

McGivney, V. (1990) *Education's for Other People: Access to education for non-participant adults,* Leicester: NIACE.

McIlroy, J. and Westwood, S. (1993) *Border Country: Raymond Williams in Adult Education,* Leicester: NIACE.

McLean, M. (1992) *The Promise and Perils of Educational Comparison,* London: Tufnell Press.

McLean, M. (1995) *Educational Traditions Compared,* London: David Fulton Publishers.

Merriam, S. B. and Brockett, R. (1997) *The Profession and Practice of Adult Education,* San Francisco: Jossey-Bass.

Middleton, S. (1987) 'Schooling and radicalisation: life histories of New Zealand feminist teachers', *British Journal of Sociology of Education* 8 (2) pp. 169–189, Taylor & Francis.

Middleton, S. (1996) 'Towards an oral history of educational ideas in New Zealand as a resource for teacher education', *Teaching and Teacher Education* 12 (5) pp. 543–560, Elsevier.

Milana, M. (2012) 'Political globalization and the shift from adult education to lifelong learning', *European Journal for Research on the Education and Learning of Adults* 2 pp. 103–117, Linköping University Electronic Press.

Millerson G. L. (1964) *The Qualifying Association,* London: Routledge and Kegan Paul.

Ministry of Education (2008) *The Development and State of the Art of Adult Learning and Education: National Report of New Zealand,* Wellington: Ministry of Education.

Ministry of Education (2010) *Tertiary Education Strategy 2010–2015* www.minedu.govt.nz/tertiaryeducationstrategy (accessed 1 November 2011).

Ministry of Reconstruction (1919) *Final Report of the Adult Education Committee,* Cmd 321 (The Smith Report) London: HMSO.

Morrison, S. and Vaioleti, T. (2008) *Ko Te Tangata,* Hamilton NZ: University of Waikato.

Neary, M. and Amsler, S. (2012) 'Occupy: a new pedagogy for space and time?' *Journal for Critical Education Policy Studies* 10(2) www.jceps.com/index.php?pageID=article&articleID=277 (accessed 1 August 2013).

New Zealand Government (1989) *1989 Education Act* www.legislation.govt.nz (accessed 1 July 2013).

New Zealand Government (1990) *Education Amendment Act 1990* www.legislation.govt.nz (accessed 30 September 2009).

NIACE (2009) *Making a Difference for Adult Learners: NIACE Policy Impact Report,* Leicester: NIACE.

NIACE (2010a) *More, Different, Better: Improving lives through learning. Annual Report 2009/2010,* Leicester: NIACE.

NIACE (2010b) *Lifelong Learning in Challenging Times: An agenda for a new government,* Leicester: NIACE.

Nyerere, J. K. (1976) 'Adult Education and Development: Speech at the World Assembly of the ICAE', reproduced in *Adult Education and Development* 67 pp. 77–88, dvv international.

OECD (Organisation for Economic Co-operation and Development) (1973) *Recurrent Education: a strategy for lifelong learning,* Paris: OECD.

OECD (Organisation for Economic Co-operation and Development) (1996) *Lifelong Learning for All,* Paris: OECD.

Office for the Community and Voluntary Sector (2013) *Social Finance and Social Enterprise* www.ocvs.govt.nz/work-programme/building-capacity/social-enterprise.html (accessed 20 July 2013).

Office for National Statistics (2012) *2011 Census: Population Estimates for the United Kingdom 27th March 2011* www.ons.gov.uk/ons/dcp171778_29378.pdf (accessed 10 March 2013).

Ofsted (Office for Standards in Education) (2003) *The Initial Training of Further Education Teachers – a survey,* London: Ofsted.

Ofsted (Office for Standards in Education) (2013) *The Framework for School Inspection,* Manchester: Ofsted.

Olssen, M., O'Neill, A. and Codd, J. A. (2004) *Education Policy: globalization, citizenship and democracy,* London: Sage.

Osborne, G. (2013) Oral Statement to Parliament Spending Round 2013: Speech www.gov.uk/government/speeches/spending-round-2013-speech

Osborne, M. and Sankey, K. (2009) 'Non-vocational Adult Education and its Professionals in the United Kingdom', *European Journal of Education* 44 (2 part 1) pp. 271–289, Wiley.

Ouane, A. (2011) 'UNESCO's drive for lifelong learning' in P. Jarvis (ed.)

The Routledge International Handbook of Lifelong Learning, Abingdon: Routledge.

Paper presented at the 38th Annual SCUTREA Conference, 2–4 July 2008, University of Edinburgh.

Pattie, C. and Johnston, R. (2011) 'How big is the Big Society?' *Parliamentary Affairs* 64 (3) pp. 403–424, Oxford Journals.

PCSU (Public and Commercial Services Union) (2010) *There is an alternative: The case against cuts in public spending* www.pcs.org.uk/en/campaigns/campaign-resources/there-is-an-alternative-the-case-against-cuts-in-public-spending.cfm (accessed 3 January 2011).

Phillips, D. (2009) 'Policy borrowing in education: Framework for analysis.' in J. Zajda (ed.) *International Handbook on Globalisation, Education and Policy Research*, pp. 23–34, Netherlands: Springer.

Phillips, D. and Schweisfurth, M. (2008) *Comparative and International Education: An introduction to theory, method and practice,* London: Continuum.

Pimlott, J. A. R. (1935) *Toynbee Hall: fifty years of social progress,* London: J. M. Dent.

Prebble, T. (2012) *Standards for the ACE Sector: A discussion paper,* Wellington: ACE Aotearoa/Ako Aotearoa.

Preston, R. (1999) 'Critical approaches to lifelong education' *International Review of Education* 45 (5/6) pp. 561–574.

Purvis, J. (1989) *Hard Lessons,* Oxford: Polity Press.

Quality Assurance Agency (2011) *Access to Higher Education: Key Statistics 2011,* Gloucester: The Quality Assurance Agency for Higher Education.

Redpath, L., Hurst, D. and Devine, K. (2009) 'Knowledge workers, managers and contingent employment relationships', *Personnel Review* 38 (1) pp. 74–89, Emerald.

Rivera, W. M. (2011) 'The World Bank's view of lifelong learning: handmaiden of the market' in P. Jarvis (ed.) *The Routledge International Handbook of Lifelong Learning,* Abingdon: Routledge.

Roberts, S. K. (2003) *A Ministry of Enthusiasm: centenary essays on the Workers' Educational Association,* London: Pluto Press.

Roffey-Barentsen, J. and Malthouse, R. (2009) *Reflective Practice in the Lifelong Learning Sector,* Exeter: Learning Matters.

Rogers, C. (1969) *Freedom to Learn,* Columbus OH: Charles F. Merrill.

Rubenson, K. (2010) 'Adult Education Overview', *International Encyclopedia of Adult Education and Training (Third edition)* Oxford: Elsevier.

Rubenson, K. (2011) 'Lifelong learning: between humanism and global capitalism' in P. Jarvis (ed.) *The Routledge International Handbook of Lifelong Learning* Abingdon: Routledge.

Rust, V. D. (2000) 'Education policy studies and comparative education' in R. Alexander, M. Osborn and D. Phillips *Learning from Comparing,* Wallingford: Symposium Books.

Sachs, J. (2003) *The Activist Teaching Profession*, Buckingham: Open University Press.

Schuller, T. (2011) 'The OECD and Lifelong Learning', in P. Jarvis (ed.) *The Routledge International Handbook of Lifelong Learning*, Abingdon: Routledge.

Schuller, T. and Watson, D. (2009) *Learning Through Life: Inquiry into the future for lifelong learning* Leicester: NIACE.

Seddon, T. (1997) 'Education: deprofessionlized? Or regulated, reorganised and reauthorized', *Australian Journal of Education* 41 (3) pp. 228–246.

Sennett, R. (1998) *The Corrosion of Character*, London: W.W. Norton and Company.

Sikes, P. (2010) `The ethics of writing life histories and narratives in educational research in A. Bathmaker and H. Harnett, *Exploring Learning, Identity and Power through Life History and Narrative Research*, London: Routledge.

Sikes, P., Measor, L. and Woods, P. (1985) *Teacher Careers: crises and continuities*, Lewes: Falmer.

Silverman, D. (2000) *Doing Qualitative Research*, London: Sage.

Simon, B. (1965) *Education and the Labour Movement*, London: Lawrence and Wishart.

Simon, B. (ed.) (1990) *The Search for Enlightenment*, London: Lawrence and Wishart.

Sims, J. H. (2010) *Mechanics' Institutes in Sussex and Hampshire 1825–1875*, London: PhD Thesis, Institute of Education.

Smith, F. (1994) *Writing and the Writer* (2nd edition) Hove, UK: Lawrence Erlbaum Associates.

Statistics New Zealand (2013) *New Zealand in Profile* www.stats.govt.nz/ (accessed 1 June 2013).

Super, D. E. (1980) 'A life-span, life-space approach to career development', *Journal of Vocational Behaviour* 16 pp. 282–289, Elsevier.

Synergia (2010) *Evaluation of the Implementation of the Adult and Community Education Professional Development Plan 2006–2010*, Auckland: Synergia.

TEC (Tertiary Education Commission) (2001) *Koia! Koia! Towards a Learning Society: The Report of the Adult and Community Learning Working Party*, Wellington: TEC.

TEC (Tertiary Education Commission) (2006) *ACE Professional Development Strategy and Action Plan*, Wellington: TEC.

TEC (Tertiary Education Commission) (2007) *Tertiary Education Strategy 2007–2012*, Wellington: TEC.

TEC (Tertiary Education Commission) (2010a) *Tertiary Education Strategy 2010–2015*, Wellington: TEC.

TEC (Tertiary Education Commission) (2010b) 'ACE funding for 2010: responding to the refocused priorities' *Letter to ACE providers*, 15 July 2010.

Teichler, U. and Hanft, A. (2009) Continuing education in a state of flux: An international comparison of the role and organisation of continuing higher education, in M. Knust and A. Hanft (eds.) *Continuing Higher Education and Lifelong Learning,* London: Springer.

Thompson, A. B. (1945) *Adult Education in New Zealand,* London: Oxford University Press.

Thompson, E. P. (1980) *The Making of the English Working Class,* London: Penguin.

Thompson, J. (1997) *Words in Edgeways,* Leicester: NIACE.

Thompson, J. (ed.) (1980) *Adult Education for a Change,* London: Hutchinson.

Thompson, J. L. (2008) 'Social enterprise and social entrepreneurship: where have we reached?' *Social Enterprise Journal* 4 (2) pp. 149–161, Emerald.

Thrupp, M. (2001) 'Education policy and social class in England and New Zealand: an instructive comparison', *Journal of Education Policy* 16 (4) pp. 297–314, Taylor & Francis.

Thrupp, M. and Willmott, R. (2003) *Education management in managerialist times: beyond textual apologists,* Maidenhead: Open University Press.

Tindall Foundation (2009) *A New Funding Paradigm: prospects for social lending and investment by foundations in New Zealand,* Auckland: ASB Community Trust.

Tinkler, P. (2001) 'Youth's opportunity? The Education Act of 1944 and proposals for part-time continuing education', *History of Education: Journal of the History of Education Society* 30 (1) pp. 77–94, Taylor & Francis.

Tobias, R. (1994) *A History of Adult Learning and Education in Aotearoa New Zealand,* Christchurch: Centre for Continuing Education, University of Canterbury.

Tobias, R. (1996a) 'What do Adult and Community Educators share in common?' in J. Benseman, B. Findsen and M. Scott (eds.) *The Fourth Sector,* Palmerston North: Dunmore.

Tobias, R. (1996b) 'The professionalisation of adult education in Aotearoa New Zealand, 1930s to 1960s' *Critical Perspectives on Cultural and Policy Studies in Education* 15 (2) pp. 94–108.

Tobias, R. (2003) 'Continuing professional education and professionalization: travelling without a map or compass?', *International Journal of Lifelong Education* 22 (5) pp. 445–456, Taylor & Francis.

Tobias, R. (2004) 'Lifelong learning policies, and discourses: reflections from Aotearoa New Zealand', *International Journal of Lifelong Education* 23 pp. 569–588, Taylor & Francis.

Tully, L. (2009) 'Adult and Community Education funding cuts', *Journal of Adult Learning Aotearoa New Zealand* 37 (2) pp. 4–5, University of Waikato.

UCU (Universities and Colleges Union) (2012) *Towards a UCU Policy on*

Professionalism www.ucu.org.uk/media/pdf/c/a/towardsaucuconceptofprofe ssionalism_may13.pdf (accessed 1 June 2013).

UNESCO (United Nations Educational, Scientific and Cultural Organization) (1997) *Adult Learning in a World at Risk: emerging policies and strategies,* Hamburg: UNESCO.

UNESCO (United Nations Educational, Social and Cultural Organisation) (2001) *MOST Annual Report 2001* www.unesco.org/most/most_ar_part1c. pdf (accessed 23 May 2013).

UNESCO (United Nations Educational, Social and Cultural Organisation) Institute for Lifelong Learning (2009) *Global Report on Adult Learning and Education,* Hamburg: UNESCO.

Vygotsky, L. S. (1978) *Mind in Society – the development of higher psychological processes,* Cambridge, MA: Harvard University Press.

Walker, R. (1990) *Ka Whaiwhai Tonu Matou: Struggle Without End,* Auckland: Penguin.

Waters, M. (1995) *Globalization,* London: Routledge.

Wilensky, H. L. (1960) 'Work, careers and social integration', *International Social Science Journal* 12 pp. 543–74, Wiley.

Wilkins, C., Busher, H., Kakos, M., Mohammed, C. and Smith, J. (2012) 'Crossing borders: new teachers co-constructing professional identity in performative times', *Professional Development in Education* 38 (1) pp. 65–77, Taylor & Francis.

Williams, R. (1961a) 'The Common Good' in J. McIlroy and S. Westwood (eds.) *Border Country: Raymond Williams in Adult Education,* Leicester: NIACE.

Williams, R. (1961b) *The Long Revolution,* Letchworth: Broadview Press.

Wolcott, H. (1994) *Transforming Qualitative Data,* London: Sage.

Wright, A. (2012) 'Fantasies of Empowerment: mapping neoliberal discourse in the Coalition Government's schools policy', *Journal of Education Policy* 27(3) pp. 279–294, Taylor & Francis.

Yeaxlee, B. (1929) *Lifelong education: a sketch of the range and significance of the adult education movement,* London: Cassell.

Yee Fan Tang, S. (2011) 'Teachers' professional identity, educational change and neo-liberal pressures on education in Hong Kong, *Teacher Development* 15 (3) pp. 363–380, Taylor & Francis.

Zepke, N. (2009) 'A future for adult lifelong education in Aotearoa New Zealand: neoliberal or cosmopolitan?' *International Journal of Lifelong Education* 28 (6) pp. 751–761, Taylor & Francis.

Zinn, L. (1990) 'Identifying your philosophical orientation' in M. W. Galbraith (ed.) *Adult Learning Methods: A guide for effective instruction,* pp. 39–77, Malabar: Krieger.

Index